ecstatic
kabbalah

Rabbi David A. Cooper

ecstatic kabbalah

SOUNDS TRUE

Published 2005
Printed in Korea

ISBN I-59179-344-0

Library of Congress Control Number: 2005927088

Audio learning programs by Rabbi David A. Cooper from Sounds True:
The Mystical Kabbalah
The Holy Chariot
Kabbalah Meditation
The Beginner's Guide to the Kabbalah

TABLE OF CONTENTS

Acknowledgments

WITHOUT THE SUPPORT and commitment of my life-partner, Shoshana, this book never could have been written. We have co-taught at dozens of retreats, and she has been steadfast in seeking authenticity and truth. She never wavers in naming things as they are, bringing clarity and wisdom. So, although I have written some words here, Shoshana is hidden under the print on every page and between every word. Indeed, that would be her teaching, to get into the spaces between words—to learn how to be with the silence, the openness, the simplicity.

I also want to acknowledge our long-term students, who have been so important in the mutual discovery and development of spiritual practices that really are transformative when applied with dedication. All of the techniques that appear in this book—many of which are being described in writing the first time ever—have been refined over years of committed practice.

My deepest appreciation goes to the founder of Sounds True, Tami Simon, who came up with the idea for this book. Tami, an amazing innovator, consistently brings the highest level of excellence to her commitment to make available to the world the broadest audio collection of spiritual teachings on this planet. She is an inspiration to many as a wise woman, as well as being a sensitive, extraordinary corporate director who, as a committed spiritual seeker, does her best to bring higher consciousness into the way she manages her business and her life.

And, of course, to the entire staff of Sounds True, without whom Tami's vision could never be realized. Special thanks to Mitchell Clute and Aron Arnold, who helped in the editing of the book and the production of the CD that goes along with it.

Thanks and blessings to you all.

—RABBI DAVID COOPER

Introduction

KABBALAH HAS LONG been perceived as a secret teaching available only to an elite group of people. While it is true that in the past one needed to have a working familiarity with Hebrew to study Kabbalah, the teachings have always been accessible to students who were interested in learning them. Moreover, during the past century, a large number of translations have been made available to readers with various backgrounds, and the mysterious wisdom teachings of Kabbalah can now be found in bookstores around the world.

There are two forms of kabbalistic study. One form continues to be dependent upon the Hebrew skills of the student, as it involves esoteric manipulations of letters, words, and phrases in an attempt to search out hidden secrets in the Bible. The other way does not have special prerequisites, for it is a method that directly links the interested student with his or her own inner wisdom. This direct experience can be accessed by anyone willing to undertake simple meditative practices. It has been used for thousands of years and is known today as *ecstatic Kabbalah*

Ecstatic Kabbalah is built upon the principal that the infinite light of universal truth is always present at all times. This ever-present light is not something that we need to acquire. That would be like trying to fill a bucket that is already completely immersed in the water. However, if the bucket has a tight cap that seals it, then it will be able to hold the water out. This example is appropriate to the kabbalistic teachings. We are always standing under an intense beam of light; however, we are sealed tight in our own sense of a separate self, and thus we experience an inner darkness and fail to realize that we are actually immersed in this light.

From a kabbalistic perspective, the body and mind of every individual have the potential of holding large amounts of the infinite light. Most of us, though, are not careful about what we bring into our minds and bodies, and we persist in a continuous ego inflation that keeps us sealed beneath veils of self-delusion. However, we can discover our inherent potential by undertaking fundamental meditative practices that quickly strengthen the body and mind in a way that the pervasive light immediately becomes sharper and more focused. A dark room can be lit by a single candle.

This book and its accompanying CD are designed to help individuals discover for themselves the power that lies within. The practices described are built upon techniques that Kabbalists have used for many centuries. They are quite powerful and yet can be undertaken by anyone who is sincerely committed to personal spiritual development. The simple Hebrew words or phrases that are used in some of the practices are easy to memorize and do not require any background. The benefits of working with these extraordinary practices will begin to reveal themselves fairly quickly. If you are willing to undertake a daily practice, the benefits will become increasingly stronger in a matter of months.

A sixteenth-century kabbalistic sage, Moses Cordovero, said: "The ancient Jewish mystics had special methods of concentration which showed them how to cast off [the sense of] their physical bodies, and thereby strengthened their subtle minds in such a way as to apprehend the sublime, heavenly realms." This was the experience described by sages who practiced thousands of years ago. It continues to be available to us today.

Cordovero also said, "If one wishes to acquire knowledge of God, he or she should concentrate in a special way ... and will then come to understand the hidden secrets of spirituality and will merge with the Divine—attaining oneness." The goal of our practice is this "oneness," the recognition that all of Creation is interconnected. This is an idea that is expressed in many ways, but it must be experienced deeply for anyone to realize its true meaning. Merging with the Divine goes beyond thoughts and concepts, but it is something that can be touched in the heart.

A teacher from the late thirteenth century, Rabbi Shem Tov ben Avraham Ibn Gaon, said that one's concentration can lead to discovering "the secrets of the chariot, [the mystical vehicle that carries one] to have visions of God ... and he will look into his [own] mind like one who reads a book in which are written great wonders." Thus we are instructed to work with these methods with the promise that we can attain profound inner visions. The secrets are not something we learn from outside of ourselves but are to be discovered within our own minds.

There are dozens of hints in the writings of Jewish mystics that they engaged in contemplative practices to attain altered consciousness. Some of these writings go back millennia. There are Talmudic passages, written over two thousand years ago, that refer to the mystical holy chariot mentioned above by Rabbi Shem Tov, and that have restrictions as to who was qualified to receive these teachings and practices. While we know that there were many learned practitioners, it is also clear that there were warnings to keep practices "secret," not to be taught to the masses.

This little book reveals a number of teachings that were held secret for centuries. The power of these teachings will not be experienced in merely reading the words. Indeed, one might wonder: "What's the big secret, anyway?" The fact is that many of these teachings cannot be taught with words; they arise only from engaging the practices. If the reader simply reads and does not undertake the practices, very little will be gained.

The objective of this book is not like most others. There is no plot, and it does not matter if you read it to the end. What matters is that you work with one or more practices regularly, for a certain amount of time every day, in a way that will help you quiet your mind and soothe your soul. When that happens, then and only then will you discover the so-called secrets, for you will see with new eyes and hear with new ears.

Welcome to the world of the mystic, a world in which one experiences the unfolding of life in a new way. It is a magical world, a heart-opening world, and a world that is ever changing.

Throughout this book you will be invited at various points to stop reading in order to practice an assortment of meditations. It is hoped that you will work with them until they become second nature. It is up to you. If you prepare yourself well, be assured that the teachings and the teacher you always hoped to experience will appear precisely at the moment you are ready.

This realization is what Kabbalah is all about. Wisdom surrounds us, penetrates us, lives within us. The "secrets" are so obvious, so close, so simple—we usually miss them. So now enjoy yourself, relax, gently absorb these ancient teachings, and work with the practices described within this little guide.

CHAPTER
ONE

Enlightenment

KABBALAH TEACHES THAT we cannot comprehend the meaning of life without exploring profound depths within ourselves to attain a clear recognition of our own essential nature. From the kabbalistic perspective, all of our physical, emotional, and intellectual knowledge will fall short of its potential when not informed by the clarity and awareness that come out of spiritual knowledge.

When spiritual teachers talk about "enlightenment," they are usually referring to a quality of insight that casts the light of revealed truth onto our experiences. Some teachers suggest that enlightenment endows one with supernatural powers. Most teachings, however, are not concerned with paranormal displays, but are focused upon an extraordinary refinement of our everyday traits and characteristics. Flying, walking through walls, and manifesting gold out of lead are interesting metaphors for the enlightened being, but what is truly astonishing is the ability to have a soft heart toward all who have caused us harm, to care deeply for all who suffer, or to turn away from revenge, hostility, or violence under all conditions.

Most of us are quick to react to irritations. We go after tiny mosquitoes with a vengeance; we react strongly when we experience emotional betrayal; we are willing to argue at length, even when we know the person to whom we are speaking is unalterably opposed to our opinion. We are fixated on physical, emotional, and intellectual issues or questions, often dwelling on them for days or weeks. We invent dramas and obsess on powerful experiences, replaying them over and over again, especially when we feel we are being abused, mistreated, or misunderstood.

This is not to say that the enlightened response is always accepting, passive, and yielding. Rather, it is simply to note that our normal conditioned reactions in relation to many of the activities and situations in which we engage are most probably not the way a more enlightened person would react under identical conditions. Indeed, the way you react to various situations is a key measure of your degree of enlightened consciousness.

People pursue spiritual paths for various reasons. Near the top of the list is the desire to become more skilled in our relationships with family, friends, and even strangers, acting more gracefully, and being kinder, gentler, more loving, more accepting, more generous people. These are noble aspirations. We expect that an enlightened person would clearly exhibit these traits. In fact, we are usually disappointed when we see a spiritual guide acting in ways that do not fit our image of what enlightenment is "supposed" to look like. Indeed, our expectations of how an enlightened teacher will or should act can often lead to considerable disappointment and grief.

A change of perspective, however, can quickly resolve this problem. My personal view agrees with the opinion that there are few, if any, fully enlightened *people*, per se, but there are untold numbers of enlightened acts. Each day we have many opportunities to achieve one or more enlightened acts, and each time we accomplish one, the world is a better place. This approach can completely change our understanding of the enlightening process. It leads to having less concern about discovering an enlightened teacher who will be our guide, and places more emphasis upon our decisions and actions, moment-by-moment, to raise our own consciousness accordingly.

Following a spiritual path is far more a way to live one's life than it is a means to achieve a goal. Rather than seeking enlightenment, an authentic spiritual aspirant is one who realizes the continuing process of enlightening many times every day. There is nothing higher than a moment of kindness. This process of enlightening does not have a measure; one enlightened moment is not better or higher than another. Indeed, the *process* of skillful action itself affects the practitioner. That's what spiritual "practice" means. We develop a habit pattern of doing more and more enlightened actions, and we become better people, we break out of old habits of conditioning, and we come closer to attaining the full potential of our natural kindness. What more would we ask of a practice?

ECSTASY

Ecstasy is one of those words—like love—that can mean many things. When I use the term *ecstatic Kabbalah,* I am mainly concerned with the meaning of ecstasy in the spiritual realms. The root of the word *ecstatic* comes from the Greek word *ekstasis,* which means "out of place," as opposed to mundane life in which nothing special stands out in the humdrum unfolding of time.

The purpose of spiritual practice is to gently and consistently move us from the place where we normally "hang out" in our day-to-day behavior to a place of greater refinement. In this context, refinement is connected with our conditioning, our normal reflexes and responses to situations that arise every day. Through practice, we begin to reflect and react in different ways. This change in our behavior actually causes a couple of significant results.

Enlightened action changes the dynamics of a situation. It affects all the people engaged in the situation. If affects how things will unfold after the situation. It affects how we, who have changed, feel about ourselves. In addition, there are a multitude of variables that arise out of this change of behavior. And whether we can realize the full impact or not, even the smallest circumstance can and will change the way life unfolds in the future. All this can occur, for example, from manifesting a gentle smile in a situation that might normally have evoked an angry response.

Spiritual practice, in this context, has a series of tiny *ekstases* that arise when we behave "out of place" of our normal reactions. We must keep in mind that "normal" for most of us is quite different from "natural." Normal is how we are conditioned to respond. Conditioning develops from the time we are born; some say that our propensities to be conditioned go back into our genetic DNA. But the spiritual principal at the base of many traditions is that our *natural* inclinations arise when we fully recognize the basic nature of our own minds and thereby gain greater ability to resist conditioned reactions.

Naturalness of being is built upon a clear sense of selflessness, and this results in the peacefulness of open arms, the sense of inclusiveness and non-separation. When there is no separation, it means that there is *no place needed* for the selfless awakened being. The condition in which there is "no place," and no ego-self, is the state of absolute ecstasy in spiritual terms.

Each enlightened act is "out of place," so to speak. This is what ultimate spiritual ecstasy is about. When we engage in an ongoing flow of enlightened actions, this *ekstasis* slowly becomes conditioned. But it never becomes fixed, never permanent, for life itself remains a constant unknown.

Keep in mind that enlightenment as a steady state of being should never be a goal of practice, for it is a self-defeating fixation. Skilled practice results from an ongoing engagement in what everyday life presents. As we never know what life will bring, we need always to be prepared to invest our highest potential in each moment. Thus, to the best of our ability, we continuously attend the opportunities that present themselves for manifesting enlightened actions. Each and every time we succeed, we change the world.

The highest teachings suggest that the opportunities for enlightened actions occur most often in ordinary daily life. The highly developed spiritual practitioner faces the same challenges in daily life as everybody else. The difference is that one who is awakened recognizes the essential nature of what is happening, while the one who is not awakened is easily overwhelmed by an ongoing flow of dramas. We can only see clearly when we are able to gain some distance from the all-consuming self-indulgence that causes us to believe we are separate and thus gives us a distorted view of existence. That distorted view causes a great number of harmful actions, false beliefs, negative reactions, and confusion. So the aspiration or goal of practice is nothing more than breaking down this wall of confusion brick by brick.

The learning program offered in this book is designed to teach specific practices that will help you experience more refined states of mind, and these mind-states open new levels of insight and new recognitions of the nature of things. The more you see clearly on the spiritual plane, the better informed you will be on the physical, emotional, and intellectual levels of knowing. The more informed you are, the deeper you can go. So, the spiritual path is not a separate life process, but is in fact completely related to and dependent upon the way you engage your ordinary daily life experiences.

CHAPTER
TWO

Kabbalah

THE KABBALAH

The Kabbalah is essentially a collection of methods and teachings that are used in an attempt to understand the nature of the universe, including how and why it was created. The word *Kabbalah* means "to receive," which implicitly suggests that the primary focus is upon the receiver.

A great deal of emphasis in the spiritual realm is concerned with teachings. We believe that if we simply find the right teacher or the special teachings, we will gain great wisdom. From this perspective, spiritual wisdom can be found in the library. Kabbalah has a very different viewpoint. The emphasis in Kabbalah is directed more to the container than that which fills it. What is accomplished by pouring a library full of wisdom teachings into a vessel that is blocked, unable to receive or hold anything?

On the other hand, when a container is open and able to retain everything that enters, an opportunity then exists for the development of wisdom. The kabbalistic approach is that every blade of grass and every grain of sand contain within it the wisdom of the universe. The teachings of Kabbalah are not so relevant with regard to their substance, for often the information is arcane and abstract. Far more relevant to the Kabbalist is the mindset that arises when one engages in kabbalistic techniques. It is one's frame of mind that creates a clear vessel to receive extraordinary wisdom teachings. Information, as such, is not the gateway to spiritual wisdom. Rather, the crucial element is the person, you, the container that holds the information.

Kabbalah has always delved into unusual realms and has often been misconstrued and misused by those who are misguided about its purpose. Some people are inclined to teach Kabbalah as a form of magic, with the implication that it will provide tools with which one can gain powers to manipulate fate. While it is true that there are stories of ancient sages who created golems and who seemed to have had magical powers, these stories are actually tangential and not the point.

A story that better represents extraordinary wisdom is of a great sage encountering a spiritual devotee who had spent fifty years in intensive practices. When the sage inquired of the devotee what he had accomplished in his spiritual life, the student proceeded to walk on water. The sage's comment to the student was, "If that is all you can show for your practice, what a pity!"

The ability to manipulate reality as we know it may be a "miracle," but it has little to do with the reason realized sages constantly engaged in practice, even after their awakening. The main interest of Kabbalists throughout history has been to understand the "mind of God," so to speak, in order to fulfill one's potential during his or her lifetime. The goal is to become a complete vehicle that is a clear and unspoiled expression of the divine will. So if a student's motivation to engage in spiritual practices is to develop magical skills, he or she is already trapped in the sticky tentacles of desire for self-attainment.

The reader should be wary of such desires. This book is not designed to teach anyone how to acquire occult powers. Instead, it is a book that describes kabbalistic practices that help to calm a confused mind and that lead to a clear awareness of how things work in this world of ours. This awareness helps us come to terms with our own lives in a way that brings ever-increasing peace of mind.

Peace of mind does not result from the attempt to control our lives. In fact, it is just the opposite. It comes from the wisdom that is illuminated when we learn how to relax in a way that allows us to "be with what is." In our practice, we learn how to engage in something when it is appropriate and how to disengage as well. Peace of mind comes from recognizing how one fits into the scheme of things, the degree to which all life is interconnected, and the realization that nobody is ever alone.

THE TREE OF LIFE

Many teachings of Kabbalah are connected with the Tree of Life. This metaphorical tree is a schematic representation of the mystical view of creation. Just as a physicist regards atomic particles as the building blocks of the universe, a Kabbalist regards the elements revealed in the Tree of Life as the architecture upon which stands all reality as we know it.

The common representation of the Tree is a group of ten (often eleven) "globes" ordered in three columns. The center column is considered the trunk of the tree, while the columns to the right or left of the trunk are viewed as polar opposites. One side is masculine, the other feminine; one side is expansive, the other contractive; one side represents the flexibility and forgiveness, the other represents the tight constriction and severity of absolute causality. Every

Fig. 1—*Tree of Life*

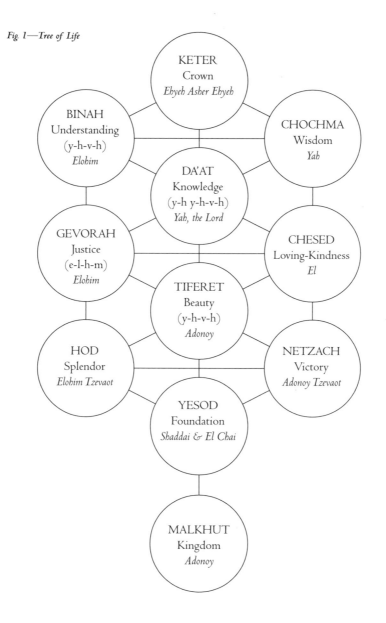

possible dichotomy, every set of opposites is represented by the branches on either side of the trunk.

From top to bottom, the Tree represents a metaphysical flow of creation, from its source to its actualization of life. It is similar to a biological tree of life that shows the simplest, one-celled organisms on one end and the most complex organisms on the other. Sometimes a Tree of Life is drawn in a way that we would normally call "upside down," with its roots in the sky. This flip in perspective is the mystical way to make a point: we must balance our normal inclination to view "mother earth" as the source of life with the understanding that the vast universe in which we live must also be viewed as our source of existence.

It should be immediately clear to any observer that the Tree of Life describes ideas that transcend our ordinary sensibilities. The globes of the tree symbolically represent mystical "emanations" that are building blocks of creation. No emanation stands on its own, but is always in some combination with the others.

The globes on the Tree represent every aspect of reality as we know it. This is analogous to the Greek idea that all of reality can be reduced to four elements: earth, air, fire, and water. The Tree reduces not only all of our normative reality but also transcendent universes all the way to the ultimate source, which has no source.

Each globe on the tree is called in Hebrew a *sefira*, which means "emanation." The idea of emanation is that the universe is created with light and sound vibrations that, in various combinations, form matter. This is similar to the way modern physicists view the universe, with elements divided into a selected number of groups. Subatomic particles are also categorized into groups that have certain identifiable characteristics. So, in metaphysical terms, the *sefirot* (plural of sefira) that compose the Tree of Life are the primordial keystones of all creation.

MEDITATION ON HARMONY

It is said that the human body is an excellent paradigm for the Tree. The trunk of the body represents the trunk of the Tree, the arms and legs represent the branches. Along the truck of the body, the five sefirot of the trunk are located as follows: *keter* (crown), just above the head; *da'at* (knowledge) in the throat; *tiferet* (beauty) in the heart; *yesod* (foundation) in the lower stomach; and *malkhut* (kingdom), just below the sexual organs, between the legs.

Each of the sefirot are associated with vowel sounds. There is a considerable variety of opinions as to which sounds are associated with which sefirot. My own approach is to follow the basic kabbalistic method of associating a sound with the place in the mouth and throat where it is essentially pronounced—the closer to the throat, the higher on the trunk; closer to the lips, the lower on the trunk. Thus, making the sounds Aa, Ee, Ah, Oh, and Uu, I show as descending from the top of the trunk downward.

You can use both the visual images of the sefirot and the sounds of the vowels to develop a strong meditation practice. To do so, sit quietly and imagine a string running through your body, going out of the top of your head, extending upward to the heavens, and extending out below your buttocks into the ground, going to the center of the earth. Imagine five light sources on the string: one above your head (keter, the sound Aa), one in the area of your throat (da'at, the sound Ee), one near your heart (tiferet, the sound Ah), one near the bottom of your stomach (yesod, the sound Oh), and one just below the base of your spine (malkhut, the sound Uu).

The idea of this practice is to bring all of your thoughts and emotions into balance. The branches of the Tree, as noted above, represent all dichotomies, all opposites, all opinions, all viewpoints, all judgments, and all criticisms. You can work in this arena to bring every tension of polarity to the central trunk of

Fig. 2—Meditation on Harmony

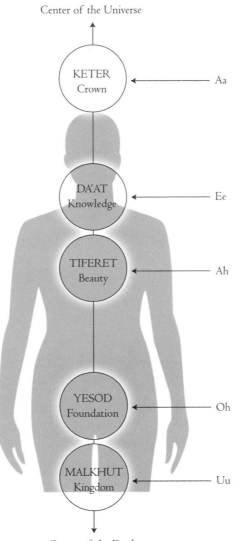

Center of the Universe

KETER
Crown — Aa

DA'AT
Knowledge — Ee

TIFERET
Beauty — Ah

YESOD
Foundation — Oh

MALKHUT
Kingdom — Uu

Center of the Earth

the Tree, thus bringing yourself into a place of harmony through chanting and visualization. You will experience this practice in a moment.

ABOUT CONTEMPLATIVE PRACTICE

This book is designed to introduce the reader to a series of practices that are structured to teach through experience rather than words. The words, of course, are important up to a point. But throughout this book, you will be asked to stop reading for a while and to play a track on the accompanying compact disc, which will help you to integrate the teachings through individual practice.

For this and all future exercises, find a comfortable place to sit. Most exercises that require imagination are best accomplished with the eyes closed. Please keep in mind that people "visualize" in different ways. Some actually see something like an inner video, others are more sound-oriented, and many people simply "think" the idea without actually having an inner vision. All these approaches work well.

Before beginning this and other exercises, it will be useful to set a small beeper alarm for the period you intend to devote to this practice. It should be no less than twenty minutes and no more than you wish to give to this practice, maximum one hour. Once the alarm is set, it will be your commitment for this day. The recording you will hear will introduce the practice. When the track is finished, please stop the CD and continue on your own.

It is best to stay in the practice for the full commitment period as this builds willpower in addition to the benefits of the practice itself. Your will and your intentions are crucial aspects of success in your spiritual endeavors.

LISTEN TO TRACK 1
Meditation on harmony

CHAPTER
THREE

Abraham Abulafia

ONE OF THE KEY personalities in the development of Jewish mysticism, sometimes referred to as the father of ecstatic Kabbalah, was Abraham Abulafia, born in Saragossa, Spain, in the thirteenth century. The year of his birth was 1240 CE, a symbolic year in kabbalistic cosmology, as we will see.

The combined twelfth and thirteenth centuries were arguably the most prolific period in the publication of kabbalistic teachings. Prior to this time, the Kabbalah was highly secretive, and there were stringent rules about who could learn these mysteries. For well over a thousand years, Kabbalah had been almost entirely an oral tradition except for a handful of early manuscripts, including the *Sefer Yetzirah* (*The Book of Creation*), a short, extremely esoteric writing that was composed completely in a code that even today is difficult to decipher.

Ironically, kabbalistic ideas first began to be expressed more openly in the twelfth century as a reaction to the highly rational teachings of the great Jewish philosopher, Moses Maimonides (1135–1204). Maimonides, known more familiarly as Rambam (Rabbi Moses Ben Maimon), had extraordinary influence in his time as a prolific writer and as one of the primary judges to whom communities turned for opinions regarding Jewish law. He was fully versed in Aristotelian logic and Greek philosophy. Having an extraordinary intellect, he tended to rationalize many of the mystical aspects of Judaism. In so doing, he became controversial for traditionalists. To this day, some Orthodox Jewish practitioners view him with considerable skepticism.

Those who reacted to Rambam's rationalism placed great emphasis on the mystical aspects of the tradition: the nature of God, the creation story, the existence of angelic and demonic forces, the secret reasons for the Jewish laws—these and many other subjects were addressed. In the thirteenth century, this mystical movement gained considerable momentum, which led to the compilation of the most influential kabbalistic work: the *Zohar.*

The actual dates of composition of the *Zohar* are not clearly known, but major parts of the manuscript were circulated in the latter part of the thirteenth century. The individual considered to be its most likely author, Moshe de Leon, was born some time close to the year 1240 CE, and thus was almost the same age as Abraham Abulafia.

This year, 1240 CE, is quite meaningful for Jewish mystics. It happens to coincide with the Hebrew calendar year 5000, which represents the biblical measurement from the time of the first, primordial human: *Adam Kadmon.* While fundamentalist Jewish practitioners believe that Adam and Eve were literally in the Garden of Eden five thousand years ago, the mystical perspective (the Kabbalah) is that there was a dramatic shift in consciousness five thousand years ago that opened up a new level of awareness for human beings—an awareness that distinguishes humans from the rest of the animal kingdom. Indeed, the full recognition of this awareness—the ability to be aware of awareness—is one of the major plateaus of the ongoing process of enlightenment.

Kabbalists agree with modern science that the earth is billions of years old. However, while science tends to focus on scientific method in fields such as geology, anthropology, paleontology, and so forth to distinguish eras of history, Kabbalists and other mystics are more interested in "consciousness"—understanding the nature of the mind itself—as a measure to determine major changes in life on earth. In this sense, Kabbalah follows evolutionary principles.

According to Kabbalah, humans today represent only one plateau on an evolutionary ladder that leads toward levels of consciousness that will transcend our current level. This potential of higher awareness is an elementary belief of mystical Judaism; it is called the coming of messianic consciousness, or simply the messiah.

The Hebrew year 5000 represents entry into the sixth millennium in the Jewish reckoning of time. From a mystical perspective, each thousand years is like a day, and thus the sixth millennium is represented by the sixth day of creation in Genesis. We see in the Torah that the sixth day of Genesis is when human consciousness came into its fullness. The implicit direction of consciousness is to transcend this level to reach the seventh day, the Sabbath day, when messianic consciousness will appear.

So the Kabbalist sees the thousand years that begin in 1240 CE as the final millennium of transition that leads up to a new species in the universe, one with messianic consciousness. The coming seventh millennium will begin in the Hebrew calendar year 6000, by our reckoning, 2240 CE, a little over two hundred years from now. According to the kabbalistic model, this is a time when the entire world will experience a paradigm shift, and people will relate to each other and to all of creation in an entirely new way.

Of course, the challenge before us is the ability to survive the next couple of hundred years. Our current level of consciousness may not necessarily be well suited for survival of the species. This is a major reason why the individual quest for more enlightened actions, each person's impact on the universe of consciousness, is so important in our time.

It is not surprising, therefore, that Abraham Abulafia, who was a deeply learned Kabbalist, believed that his birth-time signified that he was to play a powerful, prophetic role in moving the world toward this messianic view. As a twenty year old, for example, he traveled to the land of Israel to seek out the river *Sambatyon*, which is a magical, impassable boundary that in Jewish mythology stranded the ten lost tribes of Israel somewhere outside of the Holy Land. This mysterious river represents a barrier that moves with enormous force during the six days of the week—nothing can cross it. However, on the seventh day (Shabbat, thus the name Sambatyon), it is quiet and peaceful. The problem is that it cannot be crossed on that day because in traditional Judaism, travel (except within strict boundaries) is not permitted on the Sabbath day.

Abulafia's desire to search for this mythical river was clearly a pilgrimage. From the kabbalistic perspective, it was a journey to explore the metaphorical barriers that need to be encountered to break out of the limits of ordinary consciousness. Abulafia called these mystical barriers "knots" that had to be untied to liberate one's awareness. In his own description of his primary goal, Abulafia said his intent was "to unseal the soul, to untie the knots which bind it." This idea of untying knots is connected with unraveling the confusion and complexity of the world. These confusions and complexities are like bundles of tight knots in a strand of rope that was originally simple and straight.

Imagine a knot tied in a rope. It acts as a dam, blocking and complicating the smooth flow of one's finger down the line of the rope. In Abulafia's view, when the knots are untied, the natural flow can be reestablished, and we will automatically enter the realm of original unity. This is his metaphor of finding and liberating the ten lost tribes, which represent multiplicity, to return to oneness.

Unfortunately, Abulafia never completed his search. When he arrived in Acre, a war was being fought at the time in the Middle East between the Mamelukes and the Tatars. This was a literal barrier he could not overcome. He was forced to leave quickly. We learn from this that the knots keeping us from full liberation take many forms that are the conditions and circumstances of our lives.

His early journey in the exploration of mystical secrets was a harbinger of things to come in Abulafia's life. In his early thirties, immersed in special contemplative techniques, he experienced intense prophetic visions and began to refer to himself by the name of *Raziel,* which means "secrets of God." His visions were overwhelming; he often described being blinded and lost. Still, he pursued his practices and lived on an edge that was strange for most traditional Jewish practitioners; there was too much ecstasy!

Indeed, Abulafia was so unique in his practices, mainstream Judaism marginalized his work and he remained virtually unknown until the middle of the twentieth century. While a few scholars of the latter half of the nineteenth and early part of the twentieth centuries discussed Abulafia in some of their books, it was not until Gershom Scholem's work *Major Trends in Jewish Mysticism* (1941), that a new light was cast upon the significance of these eight-hundred-year-old teachings. Scholem devoted an entire chapter in his book to Abulafia's "theory of ecstatic knowledge." One of Scholem's students, Moshe Idel, has contributed a major scholarly effort, publishing a number of books that focus on Abulafia's life and his practices.

This "ecstatic" mystical approach was a phenomenon that strongly impacted on the Jewish world of the thirteenth century. A number of other individuals during that time, including Maimonides' son, Abraham, described undertaking certain ecstatic practices. Abraham, himself, was drawn to participating in mind-altering Sufi practices. Some scholars even associate ecstatic Kabbalah with Moshe de Leon, the probable author of the *Zohar*.

We can only imagine the enthusiasm and fervor shared by these students of mysticism as they engaged in contemplative practices. Many of their writings have been lost, but the works that survived—along with other documents from Jewish authors in this time period—are among the most influential teachings in the entire library of Jewish mystical thought.

Abraham Abulafia stands out from all the others in that he developed a specific system of contemplative practice. These are techniques designed to access one's own inner guide, called in Hebrew *me'orer penimi*, an "inner mover," who "opens the closed doors." This inner mover is our own, personal spiritual mentor, "who will guide us through the veils of confusion." Our mentor can be a human teacher we have already met or about whom we have knowledge, or it can be an unusual teacher who will appear to us in some form we will recognize as our practice deepens. Our personal teacher could show up mysteriously in a moment of perception observing the way a bird flies, how clouds move, the way a stranger acts, reflections in a store window, a twinge of feeling when we experience someone in pain, or innumerable other signs. Each moment is filled with potential teachers if we have the eyes to see and the ears to hear in other levels of reality.

DISSOLVING KNOTS

How do you untie the knots of your souls? Imagine the soul as a vessel made of clear glass surrounded by light, but the glass is encased in a fabric, woven in tight knots, that prevents light from entering (or exiting). You will see later that this metaphor is inadequate, for everything is composed of light—even the so-called glass itself and the fabric that surrounds it—but as a starting point, this is a useful tool for beginning meditation practices.

The imaginary fabric described above is often referred to in mystical teachings as "veils" that separate us from the full understanding of things. These veils are mainly composed of the "material" of our earliest conditioning, beliefs, ideas, prejudices, judgments, criticisms, desires, aspirations, hopes, and fears. For most of us, the fabric is a thick mat of personality traits and ego assumptions that seem at first to be almost impenetrable.

Abulafia's method is to concentrate the mind on something specific that will, by its nature, dissolve the knots that hold the fabric together. The theory is simple and direct. It is based on the principle that we become what we immerse in. If you jump into a pool of water, you get wet all over. If it is a pool of ink, your skin gets dyed. If you spend all of your time reading current events, your mind will constantly turn to the subject material that it has absorbed. If you sit quietly and simply take notice of your thoughts, you will soon realize that you have a fascinating capability of observing your own mind; you can watch your thoughts, how they arise, how they are sustained, and how they inevitably evaporate and disappear.

If you concentrate on and repeat sounds and words that quiet the mind, you will eventually enter a transcendent dimension of the pure soul, a place of peaceful calmness and gentle tranquility. In this quiet mind-state, knots automatically begin to unravel. At some point, small openings appear in the fabric, and pinpoints of light enter the glass. This light is so powerful and so penetrating, you will experience a moment of truth, so to speak. This momentary vision can permanently influence you. In an instant of realization, you can gain a certain confidence that will arise as a result of your direct experience. That is to say, when only a few knots are loosened, you can see some form of light or truth that pulls you to it. This attraction often becomes a continual urge to engage in spiritual practices that can loosen and untie more and more knots.

Abulafia used the letters of the Hebrew alphabet and names of God as primary images upon which his concentrative techniques were founded. Each Hebrew letter has been the object of intense study among Kabbalists, each has been the subject of hundreds of chapters. A letter's intrinsic meaning, the words that start with that letter, its shape, its placement in the alphabet, its numeric value (for example, a = 1, b = 2, c = 3, etc.), the numeric value of words and entire phrases, where in the mouth a letter is pronounced—all these and many other aspects are explored. But we do not have to be kabbalistic scholars to follow Abulafia's technique, for although he was learned in all aspects of Kabbalah, he leaned more heavily on intuitive, inner revelation than on intellectual expertise. We will work with Abulafia's technique in the next chapter, but first let us experience a special chant that relies entirely on our intuition.

THE PURE SOUL MANTRA

A great deal can be said about the idea in Judaism of the soul; it is not a little character that has a separate identity within us. Rather, the soul is related to the mystical appreciation that every created thing is embodied with its source in some special way. A rock, a grain of sand, a molecule of water, an ant, a spider, a leaf—each is imbued with various levels of a soul force. The initial soul level of every bit of matter in the universe is referred to as the *nefesh*, the vital soul.

Another level of soul is equated with movement and spirit. It is called *ruach.* This soul force is associated with movement and the life that is embodied in every organic aspect of the universe.

Still another level of soul is called *neshama*, which has the same root as the

Fig. 3—Soul Realms

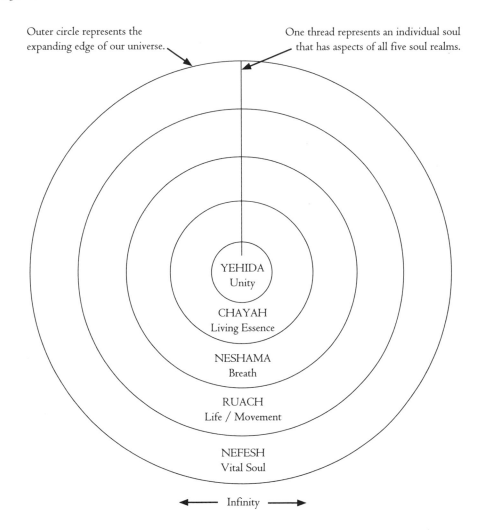

Outer circle represents the expanding edge of our universe.

One thread represents an individual soul that has aspects of all five soul realms.

YEHIDA
Unity

CHAYAH
Living Essence

NESHAMA
Breath

RUACH
Life / Movement

NEFESH
Vital Soul

◄— Infinity —►

Still another level of soul is called *neshama,* which has the same root as the word to breathe (*nasham*). This is an aspect of soul that includes within it two additional levels: *chayah,* which means living essence, and *yehida,* which means unity. The neshama is present in each and every breath, it is the source of life, and it is merged and identical with the source of creation.

The soul in Judaism is not a separate personality, but more of a mystical foundation out of which all of creation and all of life unfold. Imagine each pore composing the skin of the body of humanity as a soul: each is unique and yet each is constantly changing. Each pore is inseparable from the rest of the body. While on the surface a pore can be stained or washed clean, at its root it is completely connected with the life force of the body.

This is a good metaphor for the soul. On the surface, the nefesh and ruach soul levels can be "stained" somewhat, and we can work on getting them cleaned up if we are so inclined. But at the soul's deepest level, the neshama (including the chayah and yehida) is inseparable from the life force of the body. In this context, the soul's pure essence cannot be tainted.

In the upcoming meditation practice, you are invited to envision a pure light shining in the center of your heart. Despite any contrary thoughts about yourself, if you believe for example that you need to improve something, or that you regret things you may have done, try to bring your full attention to imagining a light that shines within you. It is pure. It is perfect. It is connected always with the source of perfection.

The following chant consists of the Hebrew words *"Elohai neshama she'ne'tata-bi, tehora he."* The translation for these words is *"My source of loving kindness, [thank you] for giving me a pure soul."*

After chanting this phrase for a while, please sit with this experience of purity glowing within. Let yourself spend five or ten minutes with this image of light shining from the center of your being. When you are settled in a peaceful mood, turn your contemplation to the light that shines in all people.

In this practice, the realization will arise that no matter what people are presenting on the outside, whatever the personality, whatever flaws you see, this being—and every being—has a pure light shining within his or her heart. This practice is to envision people who come into your life as all having a pure light glowing from within. Allow yourself to rest in this contemplation. It will open your heart.

This is the practice of *tehora he*, which means "she [the soul] is pure." (The word pronounced "he" in Hebrew means "she" in English.) Please stop reading for a while and spend some time with this chant.

LISTEN TO TRACK 2
Elohai neshama

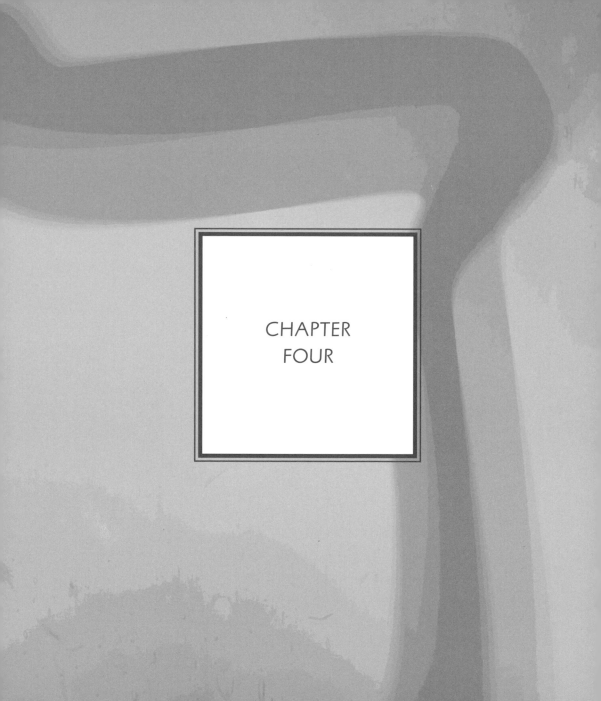

CHAPTER
FOUR

Abulafia's Practices

JUDAISM IS NOT well known for its contemplative practices. The primary focus for students of Judaism is and always has been the study of Talmud and Torah. Most people who have not undertaken this kind of dedicated study/ practice are unaware of its power as a contemplative experience. When one immerses in hours of intense Talmudic engagement, the experience is often described as a mind-state that exemplifies that of a meditation practitioner: expansive feelings of well-being, a new level of calmness, a sharpening of one's sensory experience, and a fresh clarity of mind.

Because Talmudic study is challenging in its requirement for one to be fluent in Hebrew and Aramaic, as well as to be able to engage highly intricate thought problems that can only be appreciated through the use of unique logic, relatively few individuals are able to appreciate the results of this kind of study as a contemplative practice. Yet it accomplishes two important results: a transformed mind and an expanded breadth of intellectual skills.

Aside from the study of Talmud and Torah, however, there are numerous contemplative practices in Judaism. One of the most popular forms is based upon chanting one of the highest "names of God" in Hebrew, the four consonants of the ancient Hebrew name of God, the tetragrammaton, often written as y-h-v-h. These letters can be chanted using the five primary vowels. I have already mentioned Abraham Abulafia as one of the few writers who wrote about this method in detail, but these techniques were described as early as the ninth century. It is believed that many practices go all the way back to Talmudic times, two thousand years ago, along with other secret transmissions that metaphorically were associated with traveling in a mystical chariot to higher realms of awareness.

The principle behind this practice is that each of us is endowed with divine sparks, and each person is created in the "image" of God. That is to say, the source of creativity that rests within each individual is identical to the creative urge out of which this world unfolds. In essence, the universe as we know it is characterized by Kabbalists as a "thought" in the mind of God. It follows that being created in the image of God does not mean that we resemble the appearance of God, which would be an absurd conclusion, instead we resemble the Divine in that we have the power to create new universes through our own thoughts and actions.

We experience this power when we closely investigate our own minds and recognize the continual creation of thought-universes as an ongoing process. When we are deeply engaged in our thoughts, we become numb to the physical reality in which we are standing during those moments. We seem to disappear into our thoughts, and these inner worlds become our reality.

We all know the story of the sage who awakens from a dream about a butterfly wondering which is the truth: was he dreaming about a butterfly, or is a butterfly now dreaming about him? Many traditions, and mystics in general, believe that our mundane reality is nothing but a dream that we sustain throughout each day and that we constantly create new elements in this dream. For each of us, our relative reality is our individual dream.

In addition, a mystic would say that each person is a vehicle of divine expression. Our actions, words, and thoughts act out divine providence, and some believe that free will also plays a role in this process. So we are not simply robots, doing things that are preordained, but are free agents, so to speak, who individually affect the way life unfolds. When we are confused (which is most of the time), we confuse things that influence the way the world turns. When we are clear, the expressions of our actions are also clear.

The foundation principle of Abulafia's practice, according to Kabbalah, is that worlds are created with primordial sounds ("And God SAID, let there be light."). Vowels represent these primordial sounds. Five vowels in particular are considered to be primary, with the others as secondary. As described earlier, the five primary vowels of Judaism are Oh (as in *tow*), Ah (as in *pa* or *ma*), Aa (as in *say*), Ee (as in *bee*), and Uu (as in *do*).

For Abulafia, each vowel is associated with a specific head movement, which is graphically represented in the adjoining illustration. The movements are connected with the way vowels are written in Hebrew. The sound Oh is a dot over a letter, thus we raise our head upward and then return to center when intoning this sound. The sound Ah is a line under a letter—we turn our heads toward the left shoulder, parallel to the ground and then return to center when sounding this letter. The sound Aa is represented by two dots on a line parallel to the ground, so we do the reverse of the last movement—we turn our heads to the right shoulder

Fig. 4—Abulafia's Head Movements

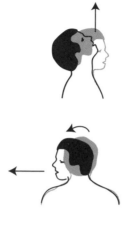

Chanting the sound **Oh**, slowly lift your head and then return to center.

Chanting the sound **Ah**, slowly turn your head to left and return to center.

Chanting the sound **Aa**, slowly turn your head to the right and return to center.

Chanting the sound **Ee**, slowly lower your head and return to center.

Chanting the sound **Uu**, looking straight ahead, slowly rock your head forward and backward and then return to center.

and then return to center. The sound Ee is a dot under a letter, thus we lower our heads and return to center when making the Ee sound. Finally, the Uu sound is represented as three dots on an angle, and it is represented by a dot in the middle of a vertical line. The associated head movement is forward and backward and then returning to center. At first these head movements are emphasized when we intone each respective vowel sound. After a short time, the movements become very subtle, but we always have a sense of each movement when doing this practice. This helps us sustain the sequence of sounds, which become fairly complicated in advanced practice.

In Chapter 2, we learned a system of vowel sounds and visualizations that are associated with the Tree of Life. The practice of that technique leads one to a state of balance and harmony. Abulafia's system is somewhat different. His sounds represent vowels, as they are written in Hebrew, coupled with specific head movements. While the earlier system was calming and settling, Abulafia's system is more directed toward developing clarity and concentration. His method is easy to describe, but takes considerable practice and commitment to master. Yet, it offers the practitioner a potential to develop extraordinary skills in concentration. The development of concentration is the foundation for all advanced spiritual practice.

When the selected vowels are used with names of God, it is as if one is creating new universes. As mentioned earlier, the most transcendent God-name is the tetragrammaton y-h-v-h. When each letter is pronounced, this name would read *yod-hey-vov-hey*. However, in the basic practice of adding the vowel Oh, for example, to the four consonants, we would derive *yoh, hoe, voe, hoe*. With the vowel Ah, it would be *yah, hah, vah, hah*.

Sitting still, emptying your mind, chanting these consonants and vowels with full focus and clarity, you are emulating the essential creative force. By keeping sharp and unconfused, you are creating pure universes of unadulterated sound vibrations. You should attempt to practice in that purity of heart.

LISTEN TO TRACK 3
Abulafia basic chants

It is much easier to learn this practice by doing it than by reading it. Turn now to Track 3. (A written description of the practice is included in the Appendix.)

COMBINING DOUBLETS

One of the fundamental techniques taught by Abulafia is to chant "doublets." A doublet is made up of a vowel combined with a consonant/vowel. Starting with the vowel Oh, a complete round could look like Oh—Yoh, Oh—Yah, Oh—Yay, Oh—Yee, Oh—You, Oh—Ho, Oh—Ha, Oh—Hey, Oh—He, Oh—Hu, Oh—Voh, Oh—Vah, Oh—Veh, Oh—Vee, Oh—Vu, Oh—Ho, Oh—Ha, Oh—Hey, Oh—He, Oh—Hu … followed by another complete round like this but beginning with the Ah vowel. This round would be followed by one beginning with the Aa vowel, then one with the Ee and finally one with the Uu.

Notice that this description may seem confusing when you read it. The logical part of the brain wants to "figure it out." But once you actually begin to experience the chanting process on a somatic level, with the body, you will see that it works much more easily than logic had suggested.

Begin by inhaling while simultaneously internally making the sound of the vowel. Then, with each exhalation, you will make the respective consonant. Always remember to move the head slightly as you make each sound, as this movement will assist your ability to stay with the correct sequence. Now please turn to Track 4, and you will soon experience a flow that will carry you through the practice.

LISTEN TO TRACK 4
Abulafia doublets

MERGING DIVINE NAMES: THE SHIVITI

The integration of the transcendent name of God with the ever-present name is one of the most esoteric practices in Kabbalah; as such it is also one of the most transformative. In many places in Jewish prayer books, when a special prayer is about to be read or a special act is about to be performed, one finds the language: "I am about to do this act for the sake of the unification of the Holy One ... bringing together the transcendent with the immanent ... in perfect unity."

The integration of the upper and lower realms is a primary kabbalistic teaching found in the Torah (Ps. 16:8): *Shiviti Ado-noy LeNegdi Tamid,* which means "I set/place God before me always." This teaching suggests that the goal of Jewish mysticism is to experience the presence of the Divine at every moment and in every situation. One of the ways to do this is to chant the above phrase over and over again. When the words are transformed through daily practice into an actual experience of Presence, your life can be dramatically affected.

You have experienced the Abulafia practice of working with letters and vowels. Now experience another method for integrating God-names by chanting repeatedly the phrase of the shiviti. As this is one of the most well known kabbalistic teachings, many melodies have been composed for it. The melody on Track 5 is one that we frequently use in meditation retreats.

LISTEN TO TRACK 5

Shiviti

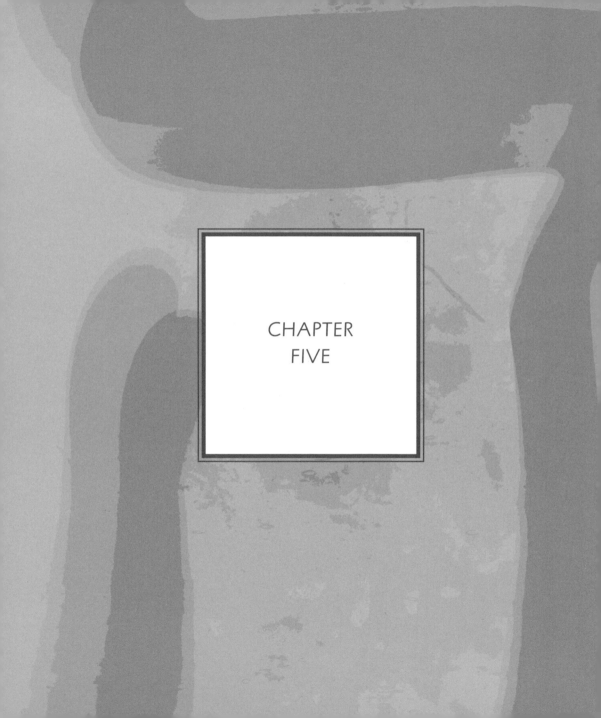

CHAPTER
FIVE

Names of God

THE ANCIENT JEWISH sages were quite precise and clear in saying that there is only one authentic identification for God, represented by the four Hebrew letters y-h-v-h. No attempt should be made to enunciate these letters as a name of God. Why are these sages so concerned about a word that would embrace the Divine? It is because they knew that words are by nature self-limiting. Even the word *infinity* suggests something that is bound by letters, and it leads to absurdities in the language, such as the idea, "beyond infinity."

If we put a name to God, we are suggesting that our language and our thoughts can somehow grasp an idea of God. We can see today that the word *God* means many things to many people. Moreover, many actions are taken in the name of God that cause incredible pain and destruction. This is precisely what the sages of the past were attempting to avoid. Their understanding of the boundless source of existence was that it is inconceivable. Giving "It" a name will only lead to serious consequences, according to the sages. They were correct. Recent examples of this tragic misunderstanding are terrorists who kill people in the name of God and victims of violence who themselves react violently, also in the name of God. This manipulation of God's name is clearly confused and a sad consequence of a belief that the human mind can grasp the essential nature of the Divine.

Many traditions attempt to assign specific attributes that are considered God-like in character. This also has a limited application. Most of the time we connect attributes that are "good" in nature: loving, kind, compassionate, gentle, peaceful, caring, and so forth. These, of course, are the characteristics of the way we would want God to be.

However, there are many negative attributes that could also be associated with God, such as: jealousy, vengefulness, anger, sternness, ignorance, strictness, punishment, deception, and ambivalence. If we attempt to disassociate these negative attributes from God, then we are caught in the dilemma that there are parts of the universe where God does not exist—the "bad" parts—and this leads to new levels of confusion, such as, "We are good and on God's side, while they are bad and hated by God." This is a terrible idea, and it continues to breed ignorance, pain, and suffering in our world.

Boundlessness is beyond definition; it is beyond the sum of all of its "parts." That is to say, if we put together all of the possible attributes and characteristics that could possibly exist in this universe, Boundlessness would embrace all of them and still be "larger," beyond all limits—thus ultimately unimaginable, ungraspable, unknowable.

When a God-name is used, we must always keep in mind that it represents only a small fragment of divine Boundlessness. There are many God-names in

Hebrew that describe attributes. Still, time and time again the sages caution us to be careful not to confuse the name of an attribute with the source itself.

The Talmud goes to great length in its discussion of the use of divine names. The highest and most sacred name is the tetragrammaton described above. As the letters do not make a word that can be pronounced, substitute names like *Adonoy* or *Elohim* are used in its place. Even those substitute names must be handled with care, to be used with considerable discretion and respect. For example, Orthodox Jewish practitioners today, when using those names outside of prayers and liturgical situations, are likely to re-substitute the words *ado-shem* for Adonoy and *elo-kim* for Elohim. Also a common replacement is the word *hashem*, which means "the Name." Thus, in response to a basic question, such as "How are you?" a typical response would be *"Baruch Hashem"* (blessed is the Name), which is like saying in English, "Thank God."

Each of the many God-names found in Hebrew literature is connected with an attribute. For example, the name *El* is associated with loving-kindness. It is often used to demonstrate a contrast between the concept of God and that of humankind, and thereby it emphasizes the idea of relationship. Interestingly, some of the most famous characters in the Bible have this God-name included in their own: Elijah, Elisha, and Elimelech, as well as Israel, Ishmael, and Samuel.

Consider the many modified names that connect El with different attributes. *El ha-Ne-eman* means the faithful God; *El ha-Gedol*, the great God; *El ha-Kedosh*, the holy God; *El Ra-ee*, the God who is seen; *El Da-ot*, the all-knowing God; *El Mis-tah-ter*, the God who hides; *El Kanah*, the jealous God. *El Elyon* is the God on high (transcendent); *El Olam* is the worldly God (immanent). *El Berit* is connected with covenants and is the God-face with whom we bargain and make commitments.

Elohim, the plural form of *Eloha*, is traditionally connected with justice and causality; its polar opposite is El, which—as mentioned—represents loving-kindness and compassion. Thus, although these names sound alike, one (Elohim) actually signifies a strict, unrelenting force that always repays deeds in kind and assuredly punishes perpetrators when its laws are broken. It never wavers in the context of justice. The other (El) has great "patience," its compassionate nature can be swayed with argument or good deeds, and it always gives the benefit of doubt. The Kabbalist knows immediately the opposite nature of these two faces of God, for El is associated in the Tree of Life with *Chesed* (loving-kindness), while Elohim is related to *Gevorah* (justice). (See Figure 1, the Tree of Life.)

When the name *Adonoy* is substituted for y-h-v-h, it implies a forgiving God; so too does the word *Shekhina*, which means the indwelling sense often referred to as the Divine Presence; *Shaddai* is connected with strength and protection, which is why the mezuzah on the doorposts of Jewish homes have the letter *shin* on it. (Shaddai is spelled *shin, dalet, yod.*) Shaddai also is connected with nurturing, for it is associated with the Hebrew word *shad,* which means "breast"—so Shaddai is at times called "the breasted God," which could also be interpreted as the "protector of the hearth." Yah is the sound that replicates the first two letters of the tetragrammaton (y-h), and it is that sense of the Divine we experience in our breath—Yaaaaaaah. We know explicitly how the source of life is centered in the core of our breath; our experience is immediate when the breath is cut off for more than a minute. Just quietly sighing, we can hear a "Yaaah" within the breath.

Ehyeh Asher Ehyeh ("I am what I am; I will be what I will be") is the attribute of inclusiveness, total interconnectivity: oneness. *Ha Makom* represents the sense of omnipresence; *ha Shalom* represents the nature of complete peace; *Ribonno shel Olam* represents omnipotence. There are dozens of other names.

The reader can imagine the confusion that often arises when trying to understand the nature of the Divine. English-speaking readers who do not speak Hebrew or Aramaic must continuously keep in mind when working with any translation of the Hebrew Bible that virtually all the names for these characteristics of the Divine are lumped together into two basic English words: either God or Lord. Of course, these two words lack the critical nuances described above, and thus whole bodies of text are misunderstood and misrepresented. Even more problematic, when the word *God* is substituted for the tetragrammaton, it is not surprising that it invariably leads to fundamental misconstructions that have perplexed non-Hebrew-literate theologians and philosophers for many centuries.

Fortunately, the practices that we work with eliminate the difficulties encountered in the meanings of the many different names. In essence, by chanting the sounds, we are able to transcend the limitations of our own intellects—we bypass the universe of the thinking mind and dwell mainly in the physical-emotional realms.

In using fundamental chanting methods, we automatically begin to purify and harmonize our bodies and emotions. In this way, chanting can make our minds calm and more receptive. Reading about or studying meditation does not make us meditators. But sitting quietly, occasionally chanting special sounds, we connect with a deeper truth, and in this way we touch our souls beyond all intellectual processes. The fact that we are working with sacred sounds does not require that we intellectually understand esoteric meanings of the sounds, especially in the beginning of practice. This level of practice is strictly experiential; it works primarily beyond the intellect—the actual results defy words and definitions.

By treating the nameless source with continuous respect, you will develop and sustain a kind of sacred relationship, a special friendship. As you will see time and again, the main gate to wisdom is to find a way to release your sense of being a separate self; in so doing, you allow a natural merging into the recognition of being One with the source of life. The beginning of this wisdom, it is taught, is to realize an enormous sense of awe of the unfolding of creation in each moment. Chanting assists in this process, as it focuses and channels the mind.

Some practitioners use a selection of the God-names mentioned above and repeat them over and over, often developing a rhythm with the breath. While chanting like this, you would visualize the quality the name represents. You would immerse yourself in the feelings that are evoked and thereby connect on a deep level with the name. This is a fundamental practice done in many traditions, a letting go of your self-image and your posturing, allowing the new attribute to penetrate and pervade your deepest consciousness. Experience now a unique heart practice with a significant combination of God-names.

CHANTING PRACTICE: RECOGNIZING MEASURELESS LOVE

One of the most important God-names that appears in the Torah is the combination form of *y-h-v-h Elohaynu*, usually read "Adonoy Elohaynu" and usually translated "the Lord, our God." These two God-names appear linked together over a thousand times in the Torah.

The *Zohar* says that the joining of these two names is so prevalent, we should realize that they are indivisible. This indivisibility is paradoxical, as the names represent diametrically opposite characteristics. The four-letter name is transcendent, absolute, and unknowable; the name Elohai is immanent, relative, and represents everything that exists.

In essence, this teaching suggests that heaven and earth are not separate. In Buddhist parlance, the identical teaching is that *nirvana* (a transcendent reality) and *samsara* (the world as we know it) are the same. This is far more than a mere concept; it becomes an extraordinary way to relate to life.

My wife, Shoshana, and I have visited Auschwitz three different times on special retreats. One's heart breaks open within moments of entering the bleak grounds of Birkenau, which was the main death camp connected with Auschwitz, an eerie place that continues to have row after row of barbed wire and fences that at one time were electrified. One of the first questions that arises for many people in this setting is: Where was God when this happened?

Shoshana spent many hours on our first retreat there attempting to sing a chant that she composed, which uses words that appear in daily prayers: *Ahavat Olam Ahavtanu, Y-H-V-H Elohaynu;* in English this means, "With an eternal love you have loved us, Adonoi Elohaynu." For many days she was troubled by the power of the experience, and the words she knew so well simply caught in her throat.

At some point on our second retreat, we both began to see things differently. The question changed from "Where was God ... ?" to "The source of life is everywhere, even here ... " and in this change of perspective, an entirely new understanding of the nature of the Divine arose. At that point, she was able to sing her beautiful chant of Ahavat Olam, and I was able to experience continuous Presence, even standing at the gateway to the crematorium.

When one chants this melody, and others as well, it is helpful to rest one's inquiring mind and simply immerse in the music. When the words of our busy minds fall away, we can relax into something more poignant than an idea or a thought. We let go into the vastness of Boundlessness and learn to rest in things just as they are.

LISTEN TO TRACK 6
Ahavat olam

CHAPTER
SIX

The Sense of Presence

AN ALMOST UNIVERSAL goal of spiritual practice is to evoke a primordial realization: that all things are inseparably interconnected; therefore, we are never alone. The full implications of apprehending this understanding on a gut level draws us out of our sense of separation and aloneness to an extraordinary spiritual experience, known as Presence.

In physics, the idea of Presence is expressed in the theory of energy. In simple terms, the entire universe is composed of the presence of energy in various forms. Each cell in our bodies is a function of energy. Each breath we take, every step, every movement, every relationship, every event is an expression of energy. It is impossible to consider that we might separate ourselves from the source of energy. Indeed, even after death, our energies transmute into other energetic forms. This idea is so elementary, a universe without energy is inconceivable and absurd.

In spiritual traditions, however, there is a tendency to transcend the normal dimensions of time and space, which are clearly a function of energy, and explore other realms that are mystical in nature. As an example, while the quality of love can be recognized in its energetic universal form, the mystic would suggest that there is also a trans-state of love in a dimension that defies understanding. This form of love does not express itself in any ordinary way that is recognizable; rather, it is the metaphysical glue that holds all of existence together.

For example, a physicist can describe the mechanics of gravity, and these mechanics can be measured. We recognize immediately that if there were no gravity, this universe would not hold together. We can determine in science just how important gravity is in our lives. But, actually, while we are able to experience the *effects* of gravity, nobody has ever physically seen gravity itself, and nobody understands how gravity works. The mystic feels the same way about a gentle Presence in which we are immersed. It is unknowable and yet, seemingly, undeniable.

This experience has many names. In some forms of Buddhism, it is called Buddha-mind. In Hinduism, it is seen as the spirit of Brahman. In Christianity it is often called Christ Consciousness. In Islam, it is summarized in the chant "There is no God, but God," which in essence means "There is nothing but God." The core of Judaism is centered on the same idea: the entire universe and all of its hidden dimensions are enveloped in the expression of oneness.

Our normal experience of life is filled with ideas of multiple things that seem solid and separate. We have a strong intrinsic sense of "this" and "that"; we have a sharp ability to distinguish fundamental differences in shape, color, form, solidity, temperature, light, and so on. Therefore, when spiritual teachers suggest that all the mental differentiations actually arise out of a basic oneness—or nothingness—we are often befuddled by this idea. Our confusion arises out of an elementary reality: we know it, feel it, touch it, experience it. The teaching of oneness conflicts with our sensory experience of multiplicity.

Imagine you have magical glasses that when worn would allow only energy to be seen. What you would normally see as a tree, with these glasses you would instead see raw energy expressed in elemental forms of light and sound. The glasses would allow you to see or hear every elemental form of light and sound covering the entire spectrum, but nothing else. So, your visual experience of everything in the world would become light interacting with light; your aural experience would be combinations of sounds. You would dwell in the Presence of light and sound.

Another essential element of energy is heat. Heat is generated from movement, and all matter is built upon movement. So there could be another set of magical glasses that could just recognize heat in various degrees, and nothing else. With these glasses on, you would dwell in the Presence of heat; your entire universe would be nothing but different degrees of heat.

From a metaphysical perspective, we could propose that the fundamental element of the universe is love. Love is the bonding force that holds everything together. Imagine what the magical glasses would reveal if you could only see love, and nothing else. You would dwell in the Presence of love.

In literature composed over many centuries of spiritual exploration, we find thousands of testimonies of individuals who have experienced a spontaneous immersion in Presence. Whether it is called God, Buddha-mind, Christ Consciousness, Allah, Brahman, Love, Light, Sound, or Warmth, there is an experience described by many people in different situations in which all distinctions disappear and an extraordinary sense of connectedness arises. All of these experiences are contained under the umbrella of Presence.

But there is one final step to this process of being in Presence that is crucial to fully understand. It is a powerful recognition that has a mind-altering effect. This step, even though it occurs spontaneously, must be pointed out, for it is easily missed.

Here it is: When we are looking through our magical glasses, we can learn to realize that there is only energy in a primordial form. But the full leap in consciousness occurs when we realize that *the one who is looking through the glasses, and indeed the glasses themselves, are the same as what is being seen—it is all energy, or all love; the subject is identical with the object.* We realize that there is no separation between what is being seen and the "who" that is seeing. This is the ultimate and deepest meaning of Presence.

At first we may think that we "experience" Presence, but that is a dualistic mindset that will eventually be transcended. One may say: "I had a wonderful experience today; I experienced Presence!" However the statement betrays the fact that the speaker is using dualistic language—there is a subject, "I," and an object, "Presence." This is a deluded experience. The student has missed the point. When we fully realize the all-consuming nature of Presence, we release our sense of self and all of its encumbrances. This is the point of liberation: there is only Presence, the oneness. Thus, the actual experience might be stated, "Presence is all there is," or, "This is It."

FIRST PRACTICE: BUILDING THE RECOGNITION OF PRESENCE

Gazing is a basic practice used in many traditions. Some gazing is done with exotic mandalas; some with thangka paintings; some with symbols-representing primordial vowels, such as the Aum; some with candles. All of these methods can lead to an altered mind-state, a one-pointed concentration that settles and calms a normally busy and active intellect.

Kabbalists have used gazing in a number of different ways. Abraham Abulafia gazed at Hebrew letters, words, and phrases for extended periods—often for hours—and this process would lead to 1) great concentration, 2) discovery of hidden meanings in the shapes of the letters themselves, and 3) a strong, ecstatic arousal when he mentally moved the letters into different combinations. A new state of mind arose as he stumbled upon permutations of letters that formed new words and phrases.

This process of contemplating different possibilities as the letters were mentally reorganized was, from a kabbalistic point of view, a way to uncover hidden codes in the Torah. Kabbalah is built on the principal that aspects of the Divine are hidden in deeper and deeper layers of reality. So when a method was discovered that revealed some of these secrets, the result—for Abulafia—was an extraordinary sense of joy. It was this practice that led to Abulafia's school of ecstatic Kabbalah.

The beginning practice is simply to gaze at a single letter. The Hebrew letter *aleph* is often used, as it represents the eternal nature of existence. It is a letter that bridges between the unknown dimensions of "nothingness" and the beginning of things. It has no sound of its own, but is considered to be the most important letter of the Hebrew alphabet. It represents both the transcendent (*ayin:* no-thingness) and immanent (*yesh:* every-thingness) forms of the Divine.

When one gazes at something long enough, one begins to see it everywhere. This changes our perspective of things. Our practice will be to gaze at this letter while engaged in one of a series of fundamental breath practices that settle the mind. Once you have read below and learned any of the following breath practices, do the exercise as described while gazing at the aleph.

BREATH PRACTICES: THE YAH BREATH

As we have noted, the first two letters of the tetragrammaton are yod and hey. Together they can be sounded Yah, one of the names of God. In Exodus, it

says "Yah is my strength and song" (Ex. 15:2), and the name Yah is mentioned many times in Psalms, such as, "We will bless Yah from this time forth and for evermore" (Ps. 115:18). In English this is translated, "We will bless the Lord;" so, as described earlier, we lose in translation the nuance of this particular name. This phrase, for example, would be more accurately translated, "We will bless and be grateful for the essence of life in each breath we take."

Yah is the God-characteristic that is the breath of life. We can directly experience its subtlety in our exhalations and our sighs. Stop for a moment, do a full exhalation, and simultaneously listen to the sound as you experience the inner relaxation. Sigh, without making a sound in the vocal cords, and imagine an all-compassionate presence of Yah. Imagine that each breath is itself a blessing. Yah holds and embraces us, Yah is our inner source of strength, and in each breath, we bless Yah for as long as we live, which is our "forever."

The name Yah appears in one of the most popular blessings of praise. Feel in your heart the expression "halleluyah!" This Hebrew word breaks down into *hallel* and *Yah*, meaning "Praise Yah!" Thus, when you sing out halleluyah, you are acknowledging the essence of your very breath that embraces you.

YAH: FIRST PHASE

The first practice is quite simple. Find a quiet place to sit, making certain that you will not be disturbed for about a half-hour. Sit comfortably, gazing at an aleph, and quietly whisper Yah in your mind each and every time you inhale. Notice if thoughts arise during this quiet inner chant. Each time you notice yourself thinking, direct more concentration to the next Yah in the next inhalation, repeating this time and time again until you are so fully immersed in the inner sound of Yah that your mind becomes quiet. In this state of quietude, you will begin to experience the presence of Yah

Within a week of practicing this Yah-inhalation on a thirty-minute daily schedule, you should find that your mind quiets significantly during the practice. The final ten minutes should be much calmer than the beginning ten minutes. At any point you may wish to stop gazing at the aleph. This can be done whenever you tire of it. Still it is useful to keep the eyes gently open, preferably resting on something that does not stimulate thinking—as opposed to closing the eyes, which may lead to a wandering mind.

YAH: SECOND PHASE

Working with the practice described above, take Yah with you into your daily life. This often begins by the end of the first week of practice. Every so often, no matter what you are doing, try to remember to experience the inner sound of Yah on an inhalation as often as possible. This phase will arise spontaneously, and you will discover that you can often hear the inner sound of Yah without being distracted from whatever you are engaged in at any particular moment. When in public, you still can continue to practice in silence. The inner sounds are actually as powerful in this practice as exaggerating them openly.

YAH-WEH: THIRD PHASE

About a month after you have been doing the first and second phases of practice, add the sound of the last two letters of the tetragrammaton: vov and hey. The vov can be pronounced as a hard sound—Veh, or as a soft sound—Weh. In this practice, I suggest that you use the soft sound, for it can be articulated in the back of the mouth as opposed to the hard sound, which requires a push forward to the lips, making it less subtle. Try it yourself. Say "vacant." Try to say it without moving your lips; you will find this almost impossible to do. However, say the word "way." This can be said with a minimal movement of teeth and lips.

So now the practice is to gently say "Yah" as you inhale and "Weh" as you exhale. Together, you are making the sound "Yah-weh," not as a single word but as the natural breath. (This is NOT a name "Yahweh," which cannot be pronounced, but the separate sounds Yah, on the inhalation, and Weh, on the exhalation.)

In Kabbalah, the Yah sound represents the transcendent aspect of the Divine, that which is beyond our grasp. The Weh sound, the last two letters of the tetragrammaton, represents the immanent aspect of the Divine, everything that is knowable in this universe. Thus, this breathing method esoterically unites the yod-hey with the vov-hey, the known with the unknown.

LISTEN TO TRACK 7
Yah-Weh meditation

VISUALIZATION ON THE BREATH

When you begin the yah-weh form of the practice, drop entirely all the aleph visualizations and change to a different form. In the new visualization, gently imagine as you inhale (Yah) that you are drawing into this body, mind, and soul of yours the unknowable Presence. As you exhale (Weh), gently imagine that your actions, emotions, and thoughts are becoming more and more clear, informed by the Yah aspect that grows within you. As you inhale, you are drawing in and spreading the God-face of Yah into every corner of your being. As you exhale, you are putting out into the world your most refined nature and your highest self.

Do not hold or extend the breath; simply breathe normally. For the first few minutes of practice each day, visualize as instructed above. After a few minutes, gently let the visualization disappear, but continue to breathe naturally, repeating the inner sounds on each breath, allowing the mind to rest completely.

YAH-WEH: FOURTH PHASE

Once again you will find yourself spontaneously experiencing the inner sounds on the breath in various life activities. You need not stop what you are doing when the breath practice suddenly appears, but be sure to keep your eyes open. Simply feel the slight shift in mood as you experience the inner sounds—then let it go. Let it arise on its own, without attempting to cling to the breath or to sustain it. You will breathe as you always have, but every so often, you will be called back gently to the imagery and the sound of the Divine in the breath. *In this phase, it is very important to sustain a daily practice, as described, for thirty to forty-five minutes.*

WEH-YAH: FIFTH PHASE

The Yah-Weh breathing practice can be continued for many months before becoming almost automatic. Some have said that this practice alone is sufficient to bring students to the highest levels of awareness. It definitely induces a strong sense of Presence as it develops.

When you have integrated the Yah-Weh practice over a period of months, there is another plateau of practice. Interestingly, one of the most powerful experiences of this practice occurs when we reverse the Yah-Weh sequence, as described above, into its opposite, the Weh-Yah breath.

In this form, you internally whisper Weh as you inhale and Yah as you exhale, which is just the reverse of what you have been doing up to now. Your visualizations with this reversed breath are quite different. Now, when you inhale (Weh), you envision the world and all of its problems; you bring it all in, the joy and the sorrow, the pain and the happiness, the bliss and the suffering. You do not hesitate or edit out anything that arises during your inhalation, no matter how terrible it may seem. Take it all in, transform it, and when exhaling, imagine a pure light.

This is a challenging practice and quite difficult for some people. In Tibetan Buddhism, this particular practice is called *Tonglen.* It is an advanced discipline for building and perfecting compassion. Many of us have the belief that we must protect ourselves, set up barriers, and avoid being corrupted by the diseases of the world. However, when we are engaged in thoughts of self-protection, we strengthen our belief in a separate self. As long as we set ourselves aside, we will necessarily be defended, and we will be alone with the illusion that we are hidden behind our self-constructed shields and thoughts that alienate us from life.

The inner teaching in this Weh-Yah breath practice is that our real nature extends far beyond the limited self. When you are able to recognize the divine nature in which we are all infused, there is no limit to what you can embrace. The troubles of the world, as terrible as they may be, are a mere drop in the ocean of the Divine. By doing this practice—breathing in suffering, taking on all the sorrows of the world—you dissolve your self-consciousness and then simply become a vehicle for divine expression. This is what you exhale and share with the universe.

WAH-YEH: SIXTH PHASE

Developing skills in this breath practice leads to a deep sense of compassion. Many forms of behavior that we think are compassionate are actually self-serving. We do things because they are politically correct or because we believe these actions will enhance our image. True compassion comes out of a full realization of the difficulties that life brings to all living beings. We are all touched by the things that give us pleasure and by those that cause us grief and pain. The predicament is that we cannot avoid difficulties; they will assuredly arise at different times in our lives. Deep compassion does not necessarily attempt to relieve this suffering; it knows how to accommodate it.

The last phase of practice is one of the highest forms of character development. While it is certainly a wonderful act of compassion to sit with the suffering of someone else, to be present for this person, to hold this person and have deep caring for his or her suffering, still this is a form of outer compassion. A higher level of compassion, an inner compassion, appears when we ourselves are in considerable pain and suffering, almost blinded in our own misery. Instead of running to block it or to avoid it, we invite in more! This is not a masochistic invitation, which gains pleasure through pain. It arises instead out of the profound realization that if it were at all possible to alleviate the pain of others through the suffering of oneself, then we are willing to take it on.

Obviously, this is not an easy path. Most of us are not ready to welcome our own suffering; we have not developed a big enough heart or a strong enough discipline. The visualization that accompanies this practice is to receive on each inhalation, without resistance, our own troubles, knowing that this is the same experience many others have had and will have. In this opening of our hearts to others, we pray that our own suffering will in some way alleviate theirs. Then, as we exhale, we visualize a divine light that has become purified to ever-increasing degrees by our willingness to accept what is happening to us in that moment.

We must distinguish here between two of the highest levels of spiritual development in Judaism: a martyr and a *tzaddik.* A martyr is willing to suffer and die for a belief. In the Talmud, life is considered sacred. One is permitted to break almost all Jewish law if a life is at stake. However, there are three areas of the law that we are not permitted to break, even if it means sacrificing one's own life. The three areas are idolatry (serving other gods), doing certain forbidden sexual acts (incest and adultery), and murder. Choosing death over being forced to commit one of these acts is called *kiddush ha-Shem*—sanctification of the Name—or martyrdom.

Kiddush ha-Shem is one of the highest states of spiritual awareness, and a number of the most famous sages in Jewish history are said to have died in this state. The main point of martyrdom is the sacrifice of one's life under certain conditions based on beliefs and moral principles.

Being a tzaddik is different. One of the defining characteristics of a tzaddik is that he or she "descends" from higher realms in order to help raise up those who are in the lower realms. So, a tzaddik does not view his or her station in life as a sacrifice, nor is giving up one's life the measure of a tzaddik. The defining principle of the tzaddik is the choice and willingness to take on suffering in a way that will relieve others. Whenever anyone is able to bring clear awareness to one's own pain in a situation and is able to say, "May my pain be such that it helps at least one other person to be free of such pain," we have achieved a level of consciousness that is identified with a tzaddik.

While a martyr is profoundly honored, a tzaddik clearly holds the higher ground on the spiritual level of compassion. A martyr may or may not be dwelling in a compassionate state; he or she is simply standing up for what is believed to be right. A tzaddik, on the other hand, is the living representative of the heart of compassion. This state of being can only be accomplished when one has vanished into Presence and there is no longer a separation of oneself from all of humanity.

So this practice on the breathing begins with concentration and calming the mind. It develops into something that is known as dwelling in Presence. And, in the end, it manifests in engaging the world with actions associated with the highest level of spiritual development: the tzaddik. We do not need miracles to become saintly. Instead, we need to shift our perspective in a way that allows us to embrace the world completely and willingly with all that it presents, in the recognition that everything is connected on a vital level.

CHAPTER
SEVEN

Seeing Through God's Eyes

IT IS TAUGHT IN JEWISH mysticism that each and every blade of grass has an angel hovering above it that continuously whispers to it, "Grow! Grow!" This is an extraordinary idea. The teaching also says that every field has its angel, every mountain has its angel, every nation, every planet, every solar system, every galaxy, and even every universe.

We learn from this that while individuals are unique, each individual gives up this uniqueness when identified with a group, which has its own identity. As each group is identified with a still larger group, we ultimately come to the conclusion that everything in creation fits under one umbrella. Oneness is the soul of Judaism.

This idea of oneness is in contrast with the enormous multiplicity of the individuality of each blade of grass. Judaism resolves this apparent contradiction—and

Buddhism comes to an identical conclusion—by recognizing that there are two perspectives: a relative truth and an absolute truth.

The relative perspective is dualistic, a world composed of a multiplicity of things, each of which is unique. The other viewpoint, however, is the perspective of the absolute truth in which nothing is considered unique, for nothing has its own enduring identity. Each and every thing is an absolute necessity that cannot be omitted without tearing the fabric of creation. Thus nothing can be viewed as separate.

Einstein amplified on this idea, showing that space and time cannot be separated from one another. Our minds boggle at this idea, for the nature of thinking itself is dualistic. That time does not exist on its own and that space can be "bent" and "stretched" is simply inconceivable—and yet these amazing ideas have been proven in modern physics.

The relative viewpoint is the way we humans perceive the universe. The absolute viewpoint is the way God perceives creation, so to speak. Let us investigate more closely what this means.

Every individual has a unique point of view depending upon a multitude of variables: language, culture, age, gender, family experience, education, socio-economic status, and so on. There are hundreds of variables that eventually affect one's level of consciousness. Therefore, there is potentially almost an infinite number of unique relative viewpoints. This vast spectrum of human consciousness falls into a single category known in Jewish mysticism as *mochin de katnut,* literally defined as "small mind."

The definition of small mind is not intended to be interpreted as a demeaning notion, for it is an all-inclusive representation of the way people see things, without regard to the fact that it includes all genius and all ignorance of human perception. So, Einstein's equations fall into the category of small mind just as much as small mind includes someone who is considered mentally challenged because of extremely low intelligence. The essential point is that when the human mind is clinging to a particular thought-subject, it is in the realm of mochin de katnut. Obviously, most of us live our lives in this realm most of the time.

In opposition to mochin de katnut, there is a realm of consciousness described in Kabbalah as *mochin de gadlut*, literally "big mind." The awareness of big mind is not limited by any of the variables described above. Big mind has no limit at all—it is aware of everything, everywhere, at all times. Indeed, it is primordial awareness itself.

Small mind continuously sees imperfections, it judges and criticizes how life is unfolding, it wants to fix things and make things better. Small mind also experiences strong emotions and is often dissatisfied and frustrated. On the other hand, small mind is sometimes happy and even joyous. In the end, however, one of the most common conditions of small mind is its sense of confusion—it often wonders about how life works and if there is any purpose to one's existence.

One of our predicaments in this life is our continuous propensity to be overwhelmed by the appearance of things and our complete immersion in the belief of our separate self. These two aspects of our lives are reinforced time and again, day after day, moment after moment. As long as we believe there is a central "me" and that this "I" engages unlimited worldly objects, we are forever surrounded and immersed in the realm of small mind.

Yet, consider this idea of mochin de gadlut, big mind. It has the following qualities. It recognizes each moment as perfect, just the way it is. Big mind is equanimous about matters (but not apathetic), and it is sharply aware of the conditioning that lies under all of our activities. Big mind is never dissatisfied with the way things happen; it is a calm, expansive, spacious state. It sees clearly the mystery of life and rests comfortably in the state of "not knowing" what is going to happen from moment to moment. Small mind has an urge to be in some kind of control; big mind recognizes that the intrinsic nature of creation is unknowable and uncontrollable.

These words may be difficult to assimilate. A better way to communicate this distinction between small and big mind is through visualization.

LISTEN TO TRACK 8
Magic mirror exercise

One that has worked quite well is called the magical mirror exercise. Please stop now and turn to this exercise on your CD.

THE MAGIC MIRROR EXERCISE: SEEING THE WORLD THROUGH GOD'S EYES

The magic mirror exercise is designed to give the practitioner a brief taste of big mind. While our normal mental state is to dwell in the relative small mind, it is possible to develop practices that briefly open the gates of big mind. Each time this happens, we get flashes of insight.

One of the key transformative points of spiritual practice for most individuals is to gain the insight that things are not necessarily the way they are perceived. A major breakthrough occurs when a practitioner develops the ability to bring this wisdom into her or his everyday life. Wisdom in this context does not mean the intellectual capability to hold and utilize vast amounts of information; instead it has to do with understanding the nature of one's own mind.

Most of the time we are actively engaged in something—we call this normal life—and this ongoing engagement pulls us back into small mind time and time again. We become habituated to our own thinking minds. With sufficient practice, however, when we are able to really relax into the recognition of the nature of our own thoughts, we discover that big mind is instantly and always available.

Our goal should not be to enter big mind consciousness and remain there forever. Except for a rare few individuals, this does not seem to be the normal result of spiritual practice. Most people who have devoted their lives to spiritual inquiry have discovered that "awakening" does not mean that we then live in a continuous state of absolute reality. Instead, the awakened mind experiences moments of big mind (pure awareness) often enough that it becomes second nature to live with an informed consciousness. The awakened practitioner continues to spend most time in the ordinary, relative consciousness of small mind, just like one who is not awakened. The main difference is that an awakened individual continually breaks through her or his confusion and insecurity by experiencing big mind at frequent intervals. This ongoing access into the realm of the absolute, even if only for a few moments each day, informs and significantly affects one's relationship with life. So, while Einstein's major work arose out of relative small mind, we can see in reading his biography that a great deal of his life was informed by big mind awareness.

There is a tendency for beginning practitioners to grasp at big mind as something desirable and small mind as something to be shunned. This is a mistake. We must come to peace with our ordinary mind process and recognize its intrinsic value. At the same time, we must use the wisdom of big mind to moderate the normal confusion that small mind tends to generate.

In the end, a famous Zen koan says that "confusion is enlightenment," and most Zen teachings specifically say that there is nothing more to get than to be at peace with the ordinary mind. This kind of wisdom is the product of insights that arise when we learn how to "drop" the small mind. In so doing we discover that small and big mind are actually different aspects of the same thing. As one of my teachers notes: big mind is the ocean and small mind is a collection of icebergs of frozen thoughts; both are composed of the same material. When the iceberg is recognized for what it is, it melts.

There are some wonderful practices that help us keep our inner waters of open consciousness warm and delightful, as we will see in the upcoming chapter.

SHEMA YISROEL

All of Judaism and, in many ways, all of Western tradition can be summed up in one sentence: "Hear, O Israel, the Lord our God the Lord is One". The emphasis of this statement is oneness. Kabbalah teaches that this sentence summarizes the entire Torah and all of Western mysticism. This is the essential culmination of non-duality. It is not referring to the number one, for that would suggest that there are other numbers or that there are no numbers (the idea of zero). This oneness is inclusive, transcending numbers. Embracing all ideas, it holds within it nothingness as well as infinity. It is without limit. Kabbalah refers to this oneness as *Ein Sof,* which means "without end." It is referred to throughout this book as Boundlessness.

It is of utmost importance for the student to deeply understand this teaching. This is the precise meeting place of Eastern and Western mysticism. Most mystical traditions agree on this point of non-duality.

The statement of the Shema can be interpreted as follows:

Hear, *not with your ears but from the innermost place of truth, that place within that is attuned to the still, small voice*

O Israel, *the part of each being that yearns to go straight (yashar) to its source (El)*

the Lord, *the transcendent source beyond infinity*

our God, *those divine sparks that compose every particle of the universe, the God-force in everything that is manifest*

the Lord, *that aspect of the Divine that is unknown and unknowable, that both includes and transcends the entire universe, a force beyond conception* is One, *the transcendent and unknowable force is one and identical with everything that we see and hear and know as reality; nothing and all things are the same!*

In Tibetan Buddhist teachings, all of existence is "one taste," everything arises from and returns to its source and never really has a separate identity.

The teaching of the Shema, while it lies at the crux of many spiritual traditions, is very difficult to grasp intellectually. Our ordinary minds function in a dualistic realm; our thought processes are dependent upon distinctions, comparisons, judgments, relationships, and rational analysis, all of which are in contradiction to the idea of non-duality. We cannot "think" about non-duality, we cannot "express" it directly, we cannot "transmit" it with words and ideas, we cannot "grasp" it, even as a concept.

Yet there is a kind of "knowing" that transcends intellect, imagination, and even experience. It is the kind of knowing that at times arises when we enter a room full of strangers and realize at first glance, before communicating, someone who is in mystical alignment with us in a strange way. It is a kind of love at first sight, not a sexual love, but a love that is deeply aligned on a soul realm. Sometimes we never get to speak to this person, but their image stays with us forever. Sometimes we meet, but it works out that their "outer" personality does not match something else that we "know" is hidden within them. And, of course, sometimes we do in fact connect on a level that feels as if we have known this person our entire lives.

This is a soul-knowing, inexplicable and yet as clear as the noonday sun, a deep wisdom connecting the nature of things with the nature of our own minds. The way we access this level of knowing is through spiritual practice, often in silence or on retreat. When our minds release old constructs and fixations, the wisdom of the soul becomes more accessible.

The Shema lends itself to powerful practices that open the gateways to our natural reservoir of inner wisdom.

SHEMA CHANTING

The Shema prayer is repeated twice a day, every day, in the Jewish tradition. Each time it is said is a period of introspection. The one praying traditionally sits down, covers his or her eyes so as not to be distracted, and quietly says the entire prayer, usually from memory. The sentence beginning with "Hear, O Israel . . . ," which can be said in a few seconds, is the central focus of the prayer. However, a number of additional paragraphs expand its theme, and the practitioner can spend a number of minutes twice a day in deep reflection. The idea of the Shema, from a contemplative perspective, is to remind ourselves every day of the essential truth of oneness.

SHEMA: THE INNER SOUNDS

Each letter of *Shema* (shin, mem, and ayin) has a unique sound. As we know, some words sound like what they actually mean, like tinkle, buzz, or zip. These are called onomatopoeic words. Kabbalists pay great attention to the sounds of the letters in each word and what they represent.

The letter *shin* traditionally represents fire. (The actual word for fire in Hebrew is *aleph-shin*, pronounced aish.) The actual pronunciation of the letter shin is "shhhhh . . . ".

1. Make the sound "shhhhh . . . " and feel inside what this sound does to you. Notice how quickly you bring a concept to the sound; it seems to have the meaning of telling people to quiet down. Make the sound again and try not to associate it with any particular meaning. Simply feel the sound in your heart or solar plexus—or even better, feel it in your *kishkes* (a Yiddish word that means "guts").

Notice that the "shhhhh ... " does something inexplicable; it pulls us out of our normal reality into another realm. Let yourself go for a couple of minutes into this world of "shhhhh ... ". Repeat this sound of shin and let it extend as long as you wish. Be in this world and feel its effect. When you are ready, continue.

The second letter of the Shema is mem. This letter traditionally represents water. (The Hebrew word for water is pronounced my-em, spelled with two mem's.) Notice once again a repetitive theme here in blending fire (shin) and water (mem), two incompatible opposites.

The pronunciation of mem is the same as "m" in English.

2. Make the sound "mmmmm ... " in your throat, like humming one musical note at any pitch of your choice, but hold one pitch for a full exhalation without making a tune. Again, notice what this sound does to you. If you tend to make concepts, such as "mmmm ... this is nice," or whatever, once again try to drop any thoughts or ideas about meaning. Simply rest in the sound. Do this for a few minutes. When you are ready, continue.

The third letter of the Shema is ayin. Two words in Hebrew are pronounced ayin but spelled differently (like bee, be, and "b," the letter). When spelled with an aleph (aleph-yod-nun), *ayin* means "eye," and when spelled with the letter ayin (ayin-yod-nun), it means "nothingness." Of the twenty-two letters in the Hebrew alphabet, two actually have no intrinsic sound: aleph and ayin. Aleph is completely soundless; when used in a word, we only pronounce the vowel that is connected with the aleph. Ayin has its own quality in a kind of constriction of the throat, which can be quite distinctive. It is more associated with a cluck than a sound made with the vocal chords.

Thus, there is no pronunciation of the ayin sound, but you can make an approximation by contracting the throat and exhaling, sounding an "ahhhhhh ... " noise with the air passing the throat—being careful not to use the vocal chords in any way.

3. Exhale the sound of "ahhhhh . . . " without using your vocal cords. Allow your entire body to relax as you release the lungs. Once again, notice that conceptual thinking may be triggered when you make this breathing gesture. It may be connected with a sigh or it may be associated with a purposeful release of tension. Notice if the mind is engaged, and if so, try to let it go and simply be in this realm of "ahhhhh . . . ".

Stay in this sound realm for a few minutes, relaxed. When you are ready, continue.

4a. Now, put the sounds together in the Shema. Breathing slowly, taking a big inhalation, allow the "shhhhh . . . " to begin just as you start to exhale, and allow it to continue throughout the entire exhalation.

4b. Take another big inhalation, and allow the "mmmmm . . . " to begin just as you start to exhale, and allow it to continue throughout the entire exhalation.

4c. Take another big inhalation, and allow the "ahhhhh . . . " to begin just as you start to exhale, and allow it to continue throughout the entire exhalation.

4d. Repeat the sequence, allowing the breath to find its own natural rhythm so that you are completely relaxed in the sounds. When you notice yourself thinking about anything, gently come back to the sound vibrations and the feelings of the body. Try to do ten rounds (4a,b,c is considered one round) with a clear mind, no distracted thinking, using your fingers to keep count. When you finish the tenth round, become quiet and fully relaxed. Sit quietly for about ten minutes, letting go of thoughts whenever they arise.

LISTEN TO TRACK 9
Shema

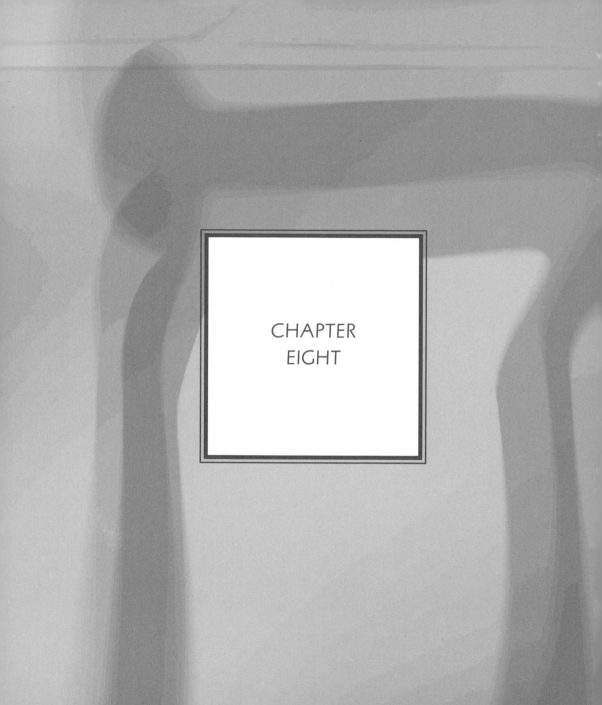

CHAPTER
EIGHT

The Thirteen Attributes

THE IDEA OF THE TZADDIK in Kabbalah is almost identical with the concept of the *bodhisattva* in Buddhism. Early Buddhism focused on the attainment of wisdom to refine one's nature and help one transcend the world. The goal was to become an *arahant*, someone who was "worthy" and "pure," a being who had cleansed all of her or his "defilements." In Buddhist terms, an arahant was someone who escaped the wheel of rebirth and never had to return again.

As Buddhism developed, it entered the Mahayana phase, the "great vehicle"—including Zen and Tibetan traditions—which is noted primarily for its emphasis on the bodhisattva. *Bodhi* is a word for the attainment of enlightenment and *sattva* is a word for being. There are two types of bodhisattvas: the relative one, who emulates the qualities of an enlightened being, and the ideal one, who is in fact an enlightened being. This Mahayana ideal of enlightenment is quite different from the earlier Hinayana ideal that is the achievement of an arahant. The goal of the arahant is to escape the predicament of life; the goal of the bodhisattva is to benefit all sentient beings even though it means returning again and again.

We in the West often believe that the bodhisattva is willing to delay his or her enlightenment in order to serve the world. This is a mistaken idea. Actually, the focus of a bodhisattva is not on putting off enlightenment but on choosing to remain in the realm of the living so as to be able to serve, even though as an enlightened being she or he is free to depart to the higher realms and never return.

While there is considerable emphasis on enlightenment in Eastern traditions, Judaism has focused more on the idea of *tikkun*, which can be interpreted as fixing, mending, or restoring things to a more complete, more balanced, more harmonic level. The Jewish mystic has always worked with three primary aspects of tikkun: 1) *tikkun ha-nefesh*, restoring one's own soul, 2) *tikkun ha-olam*, working to fix the world, and 3) *tikkun ha-partzufim*, the restoration of the faces of God, which means understanding the nature of the Divine. The perfecting of any one of these three in one's lifetime could be considered a level of enlightenment, but for the Kabbalist, all three are indivisible and part of the same package. The one whose life is fully integrated in these three dimensions is called a tzaddik.

The root form of *tz-d-k* means "justice or correctness." *Tzaddik* literally means "a righteous one." The word *tzadakah* means "charity," not as giving through one's emotion or one's reason, but as a righteous act, something that one is morally obligated to do without a second thought or a moment's hesitation. The tzaddik is in perfect harmony in every moment of life and, in so being, has the ability to quickly recognize and adjust disharmonies that appear in his or her field.

Of course, this is the description of the ideal tzaddik. Many biblical characters are archetypes of tzaddikim. Noah, the ark-builder, was the first to be called a tzaddik. In Genesis it says, "Noah was a tzaddik and perfect in his generation." (Gen. 6:9). All of the patriarchs and matriarchs are considered tzaddikim, each having unique outstanding qualities that serve as inspirational models: Abraham was known for his loving-kindness, Sarah for her wisdom, Isaac for his insight, Rebecca for her intuition, Jacob for his fortitude, Leah for her abundance, and Rachel for the hidden, unrelenting urge that pulls us to the Divine.

Kabbalists consider the biblical character Joseph the paradigm of the tzaddik. Joseph is accorded this characterization because of the story of his ability to resist the relentless attempt of seduction by one of the most fabulously beautiful women in Jewish legend. While resisting sexual seduction is the subject of Joseph's inner strength, this story is an obvious metaphor for one's ability to resist the seduction of the illusory world. One cannot become a tzaddik unless one has the ability to gain some distance from daily life, to bring an inner witness that gives one the forbearance and ability to act with clarity and acute judgment in every situation, with foresight to appreciate the full implications of one's actions.

It is said in the Talmud that this world only exists because of the tzaddikim, the righteous people who are living today. In the Hasidic tradition, it is said that there are thirty-six special hidden tzaddikim who hold the world together. We never know when we are encountering one, for they are sometimes kind and gentle but often are rough and gross in their behavior. It is easy for us to miss the qualities of kindness and gentleness, but when encountering someone who is aggressively "in our face" with abusive language and disgusting behavior, this is difficult to ignore. Yet, if all encounters with others are treated as if we are engaging a hidden tzaddik, whether very pleasant or extremely unpleasant, we can discover in ourselves a whole new potential for heartfulness and compassion.

Prior to Hasidism, in ancient Jewish literature, it was said that if the number of righteous people falls below fifty, the world will end. This idea was built upon a statement in the Torah in which y-h-v-h says that if fifty righteous beings were found in Sodom, it would not be destroyed (Gen. 18:26). Of course, we see in that section of the Torah that the tzaddik Abraham argues against destroying Sodom even if there are only ten righteous beings in Sodom. We might wonder why Abraham stopped at the number ten in his bargaining—why not argue for a single soul?

The commentaries to the Torah address this question, and a typical Talmudic argument arises, the details of which are too extensive to address here. But a starting point, interestingly, goes back to Noah, his three sons, and their respective wives, all eight of whom were considered tzaddikim. As the story goes, the members of Noah's family were the only eight human beings to survive the Flood. Thus, the commentators concluded that eight righteous beings might themselves be saved, but collectively this was not a sufficient number to save the world. This is one of the reasons Talmudic commentators give for why Abraham stopped at ten.

The Talmud divides all of humanity into three classes: the completely righteous (tzaddikim), the completely wicked (rasha'im), and those in between (beynonim). The world is composed mainly of beynonim; only a razor thin percentage of the world is composed of tzaddikim, and another thin percentage are rasha'im. Most of us fall into the middle category. We have the choice of simply blowing with the wind, vacillating in the gray areas, and not giving much consideration to the implications of our decisions. Or we can choose to move in the direction of higher consciousness.

Spiritual traditions ostensibly are based on this choice for higher consciousness. All have various techniques to assist us in sustaining our clarity and determination. In Judaism, one might aspire to become a tzaddik by emulating certain qualities. Many teachers say that when one is acting like a tzaddik (or bodhisattva), there is no difference between the actor and the actions. We earlier made the point that it is more productive for someone on the spiritual path to focus on the idea of enlightened actions as opposed to enlightened beings.

A classic book on becoming a tzaddik is called *The Palm Tree of Devorah*. It was written five hundred years ago by Moshe Cordovero, the well-known Kabbalist quoted at the beginning of this book. Cordovero was one of the most famous Kabbalists who lived in the Safed community of that time—an era about which much has been written. An amazing number of great masters gathered in one place and changed the face of Judaism. Cordovero was one of the main players in this group, himself a teacher of many master Kabbalists. He was a prolific writer, but *Palm Tree* stands out as one of his most popular works for its simple and direct thesis: one can have no greater model for guiding one's actions than the characteristics ascribed to the Divine.

While the boundless y-h-v-h is greater than all of its collected attributes, it is said with regard to the quality of mercy that the source of life has thirteen primary attributes. These thirteen are revealed at a critical moment in the Torah when Moses receives the Ten Commandments. The language is: "Y-H-V-H descended in a cloud and 'stood' with him [Moses] there ... and y-h-v-h passed before his face, and proclaimed [the following thirteen attributes]: 'Y-H-V-H, y-h-v-h, (El) Omnipotent, compassionate and gracious, patient (slow to anger), having an abundance of love and absolute truth, remembering loving deeds for thousands of generations, tolerance for one who knowingly commits sins, (restraint in responding to) rebelliousness—blatant and arrogant sinning, (kindness in responding to) mistakes and inadvertent omissions; and finally constantly cleansing away the results of the errors that we and others commit' (Ex. 36:6–7).

The thirteen attributes are:

1. Y-H-V-H as source: recognizing God sparks in everything
2. Y-H-V-H as primordial generosity: giving never stops
3. Humility: the strength to yield
4. Compassion
5. Grace
6. Patience
7. Unconditional love
8. Truth; complete dependability; loyalty
9. Forgiveness
10. Tolerance
11. Restraint
12. Kindness
13. Letting go; releasing; cleansing; not holding grudges

Following is a brief description of each of these thirteen attributes of mercy. Take your time with each one and notice the thoughts that arise. Each is a spiritual ideal, but our intellects are often in opposition to spiritual ideals. This is a good exercise, for logic tends to arise in a different universe than the universe dominated by mercy, loving-kindness, and forgiveness. So, closely explore your own mind as you read through these attributes of mercy.

LISTEN TO TRACK 10
The Thirteen Attributes

Before continuing on, however, please listen to Track 10 to learn the melody and sound of this chant (a traditional melody that is used during the High Holy Days each year). When you are ready, please return here to read an interpretation of the meaning of each attribute.

1. The first mention of y-h-v-h suggests the irony that Boundlessness precedes and is the source of everything. From this perspective, there are no actions in this universe that exist on their own; nothing is completely separate from the sparks of the Divine. This is a crucial understanding. Our first lesson, then, in working with the attributes of mercy is to appreciate that the Divine is within everything.

2. The repetition of the y-h-v-h in the sentence suggests that while Boundlessness precedes all actions, it also follows all actions. If it were purely a force that reacted according to the nature of a misdeed, then nothing would survive for more than a split second when engaged in unskillful or harmful actions. The very survival of individuals who are often lost is an affirmation that cosmic retribution is not immediate, if it comes at all. If so, where do we get our self-centered sense of judgment and criticism of others? Thus a key divine attribute of mercy is endless giving, a spacious, non-judgmental generosity.

3. Humility, yielding with strength: I have pointed out that El represents the face of God that is connected with loving-kindness. It is the yielding side, the willingness to stand back, the aspect that allows things to unfold without imposing a stern judgment prematurely. Punishment is essentially a sign of weakness. Real strength comes from a deep appreciation that the universe will provide whatever lessons may be needed. So loving-kindness and great strength lead to humility, the ability to yield.

4. Compassion: The Hebrew word for compassion is *rachum*, which comes from the same root as *rechem*, which means "womb." It carries the fetus for nine months, holding it, nurturing and protecting it. The womb does not ask questions, does not judge, and does not complain. It simply embraces the fetus with undivided and unbounded love. The womb symbolizes the clearest example of unconditional love in the human experience. Divine compassion means to let go of our critical minds and simply learn to be with what is.

5. Graciousness, *kha-nun*, comes from the Hebrew root, *khayn*, which means "grace," a result without a clear trajectory of cause and effect. The "grace" of God usually means something that is granted to someone who does not seem to merit that which was granted. We can raise ourselves by our own bootstraps up to a point; anything that occurs after that happens by grace alone. If it is the nature of the Divine to grant blessings without necessarily requiring a cause, it behooves us to explore this attribute. We are invited—and perhaps obligated—to take the first step toward reconciliation without necessarily requiring a sign.

6. Patience, slowness to anger: Even when faced with an act that seems so much to merit our angry response, we must once again consider that if Boundlessness can put up with it, why can't we? When we look closely at our own anger, it is usually connected with things like a) a sense of powerlessness, b) desire to control, c) irritability, d) strong judgment, e) frustration, f) attitude, and g) self-righteousness. In every instance, the core of our anger lies in the midst of our ego-identity, which says, "I am right." The ability to step away from that ego-core and appreciate how we are connected with the variety of life that surrounds us is a major plateau one can attain during the spiritual quest.

7. Abundance of love: Some of us believe that we have a limited capacity to love. As the merits of mercy begin to overflow into each other, however, we are reminded that there is no limit to love. It is true that we sometimes get tired and must get some rest. But the idea of love's abundance teaches us that we need not have a poverty mentality when it comes to love; we do not have to maintain boundaries that define who we are in terms of who we love or who loves us.

8. Loyalty, absolute truth: The Hebrew word for truth is *ehmet*, spelled aleph, mem, tav, which represent the first, middle, and last letters of the alphabet. The interpretation of this idea is that absolute truth covers A to Z

without any exclusions. What kind of truth is this? It is a truth in which we have total confidence, a truth that we can always count on.

Absolute truth is something beyond ordinary thought, it rests in a deeper knowing. Knowing on this level yields an assurance that something is one hundred percent dependable. Very few things fit into this category. One is death; nothing lives forever. This is an absolute truth. Another is movement; no physical matter exists without movement. Another is heat; all movement is associated with some level of heat. And one is love. Although impossible to measure, the universe is built on love—not ordinary human love but a transcendent love that is the source of life.

9. Forgiveness, remembering kindness for thousands of generations: We usually forget small kindnesses within a few days. A major attribute of divine mercy is the continuous "loyalty" Boundlessness shows for the creation. The biblical metaphor for this is represented in the rainbow that appears after the Flood, when Elohim makes a promise, a covenant, to Noah that life on earth will never again be destroyed (Gen. 9:8–17). The implication is that the God-face of justice is promising tolerance and mercy in its judgment of the human condition. This idea is an added factor that Western tradition brings to the Eastern idea of karma, suggesting that while the retribution of perfect karma might lead to the destruction of humanity, the mercy of divine compassion is innately forgiving.

10. Tolerance, forgiving one who knowingly exhibits asocial behavior: Every community and every society has its own rules and norms of social behavior; what is acceptable and what is not. We know that there are times when flaunting behavioral norms is exactly what is needed for a society. However, on the highest level, this teaching of forgiving certain behavior is more focused on the kinds of things that might be dangerous to a community: drunken driving, excessively exceeding a speed limit, robbery, physical abuse, and so forth.

Forgiveness in this context does not mean that we let criminals walk the streets, but it is directed more toward how we feel about the criminal. When the pope visits his potential assassin in the hospital or a political leader commutes the sentence of his enemy, this is a special kind of forgiveness. Balancing the use of restraint while at the same time protecting the community is a major challenge. Forgiveness helps us make tough decisions from a cool, openhearted place.

11. Restraint in responding with anger to blatant and arrogant destructive behavior is an even greater challenge. There are people who go out of their way to bring pain and suffering into the world. They at times range along the border of insanity. They hate and dare us to hate them back. Yet the boundless source of mercy has given them the breath of life and, by definition, continues to support their lives in every new breath they take. This is a conundrum, a paradox, an impossible situation for most of us to consider. How could Hitler and Stalin live as long as they did, considering the millions of lives each man destroyed? This is not an easy goal to which one can aspire. Look closely into your heart on this question. When we hate someone, who does it hurt?

12. Kindness in response to mistakes or inadvertent omissions is a relatively easy test for most people compared to the previous quality of restraint in the face of intentional wrong doing. Most so-called sins, unskillful actions, are caused through ignorance, dullness of mind, and ordinary lack of awareness. We often do not consider the implications of our actions—we destroy the environment, we overrun and trample down nature, we pollute, we kill, we excessively consume, we are greedy, we harm others inadvertently, we think of ourselves first, and on and on. It is a miracle that mother earth puts up with us.

Even though we can be forgiving of some levels of ignorance, it does not mean or suggest that we must remain passive in acceptance. We are vehicles of divine expression, and, as noted earlier, our actions reverberate forever into the future. It may be a long, slow process, but it can and must be accomplished with a certain degree of respect and wisdom.

13. Releasing, constantly cleansing away our errors and those of others: The divine quality regarding kindness is to remember it for thousands of generations. Just the opposite is true for attending harmful actions. In this instance, the slate is rapidly wiped clean again and again. Remembering the good in people and not their negative attributes is a key aspect for opening the heart. We cannot develop loving-kindness and authentic compassion as long as we hold on to our critical views—both self-critical and critical of others. We must learn how to quickly clean up our own messes and even clean up the mess others make. That is to say, we must learn to not hold on. Negative ideas can readily be erased; we can simply let them go from our minds. If we are not able to do so, we carry the pain and judgment in our hearts, and it locks us once again in our self-righteousness.

The teaching of emulating the thirteen attributes is a powerful path for building character, which is called *tikkun ha-middot,* mending one's personality and traits. Each of the points of guidance given above is a spiritual path in itself. It is suggested to pick one only and work with it for months, years, or perhaps a lifetime. Mastering just one of these attributes would be enough to pull the practitioner into a new state of mind and would provide a path for one to engage in actions that would bring one's inner tzaddik out to the world.

These final practices bring this book to an end. The reader now has in hand a compilation of some of the most esoteric kabbalistic techniques available today. Please keep in mind that simply knowing how to do these practices is not sufficient to gain new insights and clarity. One needs to be proficient in actual practice of one or more of the techniques for any benefit to accrue. A certain dedication and devotion is required for advancement on any spiritual path. Kabbalah is no different.

So, may you be blessed to have the fortitude and the will to discover the hidden powers within yourself through these and other practices and may you shine with the light of Boundlessness so that your life and the lives of those around you will be filled with wisdom and compassion, now and forevermore.

Appendix

ABULAFIA'S PURE SOUND PRACTICE
The Oh Sound

1a. Imagine that you want to make a pure Oh sound. Now do it, chanting Oh on a full exhalation. Notice your mind. Each time it drifts, gently come back to the sounding of Oh. Feel where this sound vibrates in your body. Continue chanting the Oh sound three times, completely covering the entire exhalation with the sound.

1b. Continue making the Oh sound three more times, but as you are sounding the vowel, *slowly and gently raise your face and head* a few inches, as if you are looking up at the twelve on a large clock in front of you. Return to center as each exhalation comes to an end, so you will be moving your head three times, once on each exhalation. Now rest quietly for a few moments.

The Ah Sound

2a. Imagine you want to make a pure Ah sound. Chant Ah for a full exhalation. Each time the mind drifts, gently bring your consciousness back to the sounding of Ah. Notice where this sound vibrates in your body. Continue with three Ah sounds, completely covering the entire exhalation with the sound.

2b. As you are sounding Ah three more times, *slowly and gently move your head and face* toward your left shoulder as if looking at nine o'clock on a large clock in front of you. Return to center as each exhalation comes to an end, so you will be moving your hear three times, once on each exhalation. Now rest quietly for a few moments.

The Aa Sound

3a. Repeat 2a for the pure Aa sound.

3b. Repeat 2b for the Aa sound, this time *moving your head toward the right shoulder* (three o'clock) and returning to center on each exhalation.

The Ee Sound

4a. Repeat 2a for the pure Ee sound.

4b. Repeat 2b for the Ee sound, this time *moving your head down toward the floor* (six o'clock) and returning to center on each exhalation.

The Uu Sound

5a. Repeat 2a for the pure Uu sound.

5b. Repeat 2b, this time with two movements: First, *push the head gently forward, looking forward,* as if moving the head into the middle of the clock. Next, *pull the head back to center and continue pulling back slightly behind center.* Finally, return to center. Both forward and backward and then returning to center are all done on each exhalation while simultaneously sounding the Uu.

Thus, we have five sounding vowels and six directions: up, left, right, down, forward and back, representing the six directions of space. During this practice, we become the center of the creation of a multitude of pure universes in all directions. This is very powerful, deeply settling, with extraordinary benefits on the level of purification.

REPEATING THE SEQUENCE

The order in which the head motions are described above is a sequence that in Abulafia practice is always followed: up, left, right, down, forward, and backward. In addition, these head movements are always associated with the vowel sounds: Oh (up), Ah (left), Aa (right), Ee (down), and Uu (forward and backward).

Now add the y-h-v-h, doing a round of vowels for each consonant: yoh, yah, yay, yee, yu; ho, hah, hey, he, hu; vo, vah, vay, vee, vu; and finally repeating ho, hah, hey, he, hu.

Practice this sequence of head movements and make the associated sounds, one per exhalation, for at least ten minutes, extending each exhalation to comfortable lengths. Listen to the sound of your own voice, feel the internal vibrations as the sound shifts, and allow the mind to rest as much as possible.

The important part of this initial process is to embody the sounds and head movements in a way that the sequence becomes natural and automatic. The head movements themselves should become increasingly subtle, so as not to make yourself dizzy, but they should always be done in some way, even if only an inch or so of each movement. It will not take long before you will not have to refer to the chart, but will in fact have an automatic ingrained relationship with the sounds and head movements.

VOCAL CHANTING AND SILENT CHANTING

Practice this process each day for at least fifteen minutes, but no longer than forty-five minutes. When you feel comfortable doing this sequence with your eyes closed, you can alternate vocal chanting with silent internal chanting, in which you continue to hear the sounds in your mind but you do not vocalize them.

While vocal chanting can only be accomplished on exhalations, internal silent chanting can easily be extended to both inhalations and exhalations. When vocalizing, be sure to start the sound precisely at the moment you begin to exhale and to coordinate the completion of the sound with the end of the exhalation. When shifting to silent chanting, it is still important to synchronize the inner sound with the exact moments of beginning and ending each inhalation and exhalation, to the best of your ability. The object is to immerse oneself in the experience of the breath and its sound.

One way to do silent chanting is simply to follow the sequence of consonants combined with the regular sequence of vowels. There are numerous possibilities for determining which of many variations you will undertake. See the following charts.

VARIATIONS ON ABULAFIA'S Y-H-V-H
BREATH PRACTICE *(reading down each column)*
(Notice that each column could switch exhalations for inhalations and could be read from the bottom up instead of the top down; thus each column represents four possible variations, giving a total of sixteen variations. Column A is the easiest; Column C is the most difficult.)

(Keep in mind to minimally move the head according to the inner vowel sound: Oh (up), Ah (left), Aa (right), Ee (down), Uu (forward and backward).

		A	B	C
Inhale ...	1	Yoh	Yoh	Yoh
Exhale ...	2	Yah	Ho	Ha
Inhale ...	3	Yay	Voh	Vay
Exhale ...	4	Yee	Ho	He
Inhale ...	5	You	Yah	You
Exhale ...	6	Ho	Ha	Ho
Inhale ...	7	Ha	Vah	Vah
Exhale ...	8	Hey	Ha	Hey
Inhale ...	9	He	Yay	Yee
Exhale ...	10	Hu	Hey	Hu
Inhale ...	11	Voh	Vay	Voh
Exhale ...	12	Vah	Hey	Ha
Inhale ...	13	Vay	Yee	Yay
Exhale ...	14	Vee	He	He
Inhale ...	15	Vu	Vee	Vu
Exhale ...	16	Ho	He	Ho
Inhale ...	17	Ha	You	Yah
Exhale ...	18	Hey	Hu	Hey
Inhale ...	19	He	Vu	Vee
Exhale ...	20	Hu	Hu	Hu

ABULAFIA'S BREATH AND CHANTING
PRACTICE WITH DOUBLETS

Each doublet is made up of an initial vowel, to be whispered internally on each inhalation, followed by a consonant on the exhalation. We will give here only the easiest form. There are many possible variations that the advanced practitioner will be able to work out on his or her own. Keep in mind to minimally move the head according to the inner vowel sound: Oh (up), Ah (left), Aa (right), Ee (down), Uu (forward and backward).

Y-H-V-H doublet sequence beginning with the vowel Oh.

Instructions: Read the columns vertically, top to bottom, first all of A, then B, C and D. Inhale the sound Oh silently, exhale and vocalize the respective vowel sound in a quiet whisper. Breathe normally, do not rush or intentionally lengthen the breath. Eventually the entire practice can be accomplished silently. When the Oh sequence is completed as shown, continue with the Ah sequence on next page.

	A	B	C	D
Inhale	Oh	Oh	Oh	Oh
Exhale	Yoh	Ho	Voh	Ho
Inhale	Oh	Oh	Oh	Oh
Exhale	Yah	Ha	Vah	Ha
Inhale	Oh	Oh	Oh	Oh
Exhale	Yay	Hay	Vay	Hay
Inhale	Oh	Oh	Oh	Oh
Exhale	Yee	He	Vee	He
Inhale	Oh	Oh	Oh	Oh
Exhale	You	Hu	Vu	Hu

Y-H-V-H doublet sequence beginning with the vowel Ah.

	A	B	C	D
Inhale	Ah	Ah	Ah	Ah
Exhale	Yoh	Ho	Voh	Ho
Inhale	Ah	Ah	Ah	Ah
Exhale	Yah	Ha	Vah	Ha
Inhale	Ah	Ah	Ah	Ah
Exhale	Yay	Hay	Vay	Hay
Inhale	Ah	Ah	Ah	Ah
Exhale	Yee	He	Vee	He
Inhale	Ah	Ah	Ah	Ah
Exhale	You	Hu	Vu	Hu

Y-H-V-H doublet sequences beginning with the vowels Aa, Ee and Uu.

After completing the Ah sequence, the practice continues with an Aa sequence, simply substituting Aa as the vowel sound, then an Ee sequence and finally a Uu sequence. The completion of the Uu sequence is considered one full round.

Many students practice until they are able to do a full round at the beginning of each meditation period. This requires considerable concentration and significantly deepens one's practice when a round is accomplished without mistakes. When the above sequence is mastered, new sequences that are more challenging can be developed by the student.

About the Author

RABBI DAVID A. COOPER has been called "one of today's leading teachers of Jewish meditation." He is an active student of the world's great spiritual traditions and is the author of many books, including *Three Gates to Meditation Practice* (Skylight Paths), *A Heart of Stillness* (Skylight Paths), *Silence, Simplicity, and Solitude* (Skylight Paths), and *The Handbook of Jewish Meditation Practices* (Jewish Lights). His book *God Is a Verb: Kabbalah and the Practice of Mystical Judaism* (Riverhead/ Putnam) has been highly acclaimed and was nominated for the National Jewish Book Award. It has sold over 100,000 copies and has been translated into several languages. Cooper and his wife, Shoshana, lead Jewish meditation retreats nationwide throughout the year.

Rabbi Cooper does not take individual students, but he can be engaged to teach weekend intensives and retreats in meditation and Kabbalah. His web site is www.rabbidavidcooper.com, and he can be reached at davidcoop99@yahoo.com, but be advised he is often on extended retreat and may be slow to respond to inquiries.

SOUNDS TRUE was founded with a clear vision: to disseminate spiritual wisdom. Located in Boulder, Colorado, Sounds True publishes teaching programs that are designed to educate, uplift, and inspire. With more than 600 titles available, we work with many of the leading spiritual teachers, thinkers, healers, and visionary artists of our time.

For a free catalog or for more information on audio programs by Rabbi David A. Cooper, please contact Sounds True via the World Wide Web at www.soundstrue.com, call us toll free at 800-333-9185, or write:

The Sounds True Catalog
PO Box 8010
Boulder CO 80306